LLEWELLYN'S
Tarot
Reader
2006

Featuring

Ruth Ann and Wald Amberstone, Arnell Ando,
Nina Lee Braden, Lee Bursten, Bonnie Cehovet, Elizabeth
Genco, Mary K. Greer, Elizabeth Hazel, Christine Jette,
Corrine Kenner, Edain McCoy, Mark McElroy, Errol
McLendon, Leeda Alleyn Pacotti, Rachel Pollack,
Janina Renee, Valerie Sim, Thalassa, James Wells,
Diane Wilkes, and Winter Wren

Editing/Design by K. M. Brielmaier
Cover Design by Kevin R. Brown
Interior Art by Nyease Somersett
Art Direction by Lynne Menturweck

Illustrations from *The Universal Tarot* reproduced by permission of Lo Scarabeo. Copyright 2003 by Lo Scarabeo.

Illustrations from *The Gay Tarot* by Lee Bursten and Antonella Platano reproduced by permission of Lo Scarabeo. Copyright 2004 by Lo Scarabeo.

Illustrations from *The Pagan Tarot* by Gina M. Pace, Luca Raimondo, and Cristiano Spadoni reproduced by permission of Lo Scarabeo. Copyright 2004 by Lo Scarabeo.

Illustrations from *The Baroque Bohemian Cats' Tarot* reproduced by permission. Copyright 2004 by Karen Mahony and Alex Ukolov.

Illustrations of the Ace of Cups and the Three of Pentacles on pages 175 and 178 are based on those contained in *The Pictorial Key to the Tarot* by Arthur Edward Waite, published by William Rider & Son Ltd., London, 1911.

Medieval Enchantment: The Nigel Jackson Tarot, Victoria Regina Tarot, Ship of Fools Tarot, Legend: The Arthurian Tarot, Faery Wicca Tarot, The Gilded Tarot, The Celtic Dragon Tarot, The Quest Tarot, Tarot of the Dead, The Witches Tarot, and *The Bright Idea Deck* all © Llewellyn Worldwide. Images may not be reproduced in any form without written permission from the publisher.

You can order Llewellyn annuals and books from *New Worlds*, Llewellyn's magazine catalog. To request a free copy of the catalog, call toll-free 1-877-NEW-WRLD, or visit http://subscriptions.llewellyn.com.

✱ ☆ ✱ ☆ ✱ ☆ ✱ ☆ ✱ ☆ ✱ ☆ ✱ ☆ ✱

Table of Contents

The Fool: Tools for the Journey

The Magician: Practical Applications

The Wheel: 2006 Almanac

✹ ☆ ✹ ☆ ✹ ☆ ✹ ☆ ✹ ☆ ✹ ☆ ✹ ☆ ✹

The Hermit: For Further Study

Judgment: Deck Reviews

The World: Spreads

About the Authors

Ruth Ann and Wald Amberstone are well-known in the tarot community as highly creative and original teachers. They are founders of the Tarot School and authors of *The Tarot School Correspondence Course* and *Tarot Tips: 78 Practical Techniques to Enhance Your Reading Skills*. They are also the creators of the Readers Studio, an annual national conference for tarot professionals.

Arnell Ando is a Jungian-based Expressive Arts Therapist. She has created three tarot decks thus far, including *Transformational Tarot* and *Hero's Journey*, which she has been handcrafting for clients since 1994. She conducts art and tarot workshops in San Diego and at various symposiums. You can view Arnell's art, decks, and a line of custom-made miniature occult shops, or read her various articles, at www.arnellart.com.

Nina Lee Braden is developing a spiritual teaching circle based on tarot and astrology called "78 Faces of Divinity." She knows not what the future holds, but she knows that tarot's seventy-eight faces of divinity will lead her through her journey into the future. She is the proud mother of two grown daughters.

Lee Bursten is the creator and author of the *Gay Tarot*, and is writing the accompanying text for a new tarot project by artist Ciro Marchetti. He has written many tarot deck reviews for the Tarot Passages website, and has served as a professional tarot reader and forum moderator for the Aeclectic website.

Bonnie Cehovet is a professional tarot reader, Reiki master, and writer living in the Pacific Northwest. She is a cofounder of the World Tarot Network, serves as vice president and director of certification for the American Board for Tarot Certification, and has served in various capacities with the American Tarot Association.

Elizabeth Genco is a systems engineer, fiddle player, tarot enthusiast, and writer, though not necessarily in that order. Her online magazine, PLATFORM, is about her experiences as a busker in the

New York City subways. She divides her time between New York City and Los Angeles.

Mary K. Greer is an author and teacher specializing in methods of self-exploration and transformation. She is featured at tarot conferences and symposia in the United States and abroad. Active in several tarot associations and internet discussion groups, she teaches and writes for the women's and Pagan communities, and is an Archpriestess/Hierophant in the Fellowship of Isis. Tools and Rites of Transformation (T.A.R.O.T.) is a learning center founded and directed by Mary for the study of divination, women's mysteries, and the transformative arts. Her books include *Understanding the Tarot Court* with Tom Tadfor Little, *The Complete Book of Tarot Reversals, Tarot for Your Self: A Workbook for Personal Transformation, The Essence of Magic: Tarot, Ritual, and Aromatherapy, Tarot Mirrors: Reflections of Personal Meaning,* and *Tarot Constellations: Patterns of Personal Destiny.*

Elizabeth Hazel is the author of *Tarot Decoded: Understanding and Using Dignities and Correspondences,* the first primer of tarot dignities. She has been described as the Dean of Tarot-Astrology, and enjoys developing new techniques for merging these mystic arts. Liz is working on a follow-up book that digs more deeply into connections between the stars and cards. She is an award-winning performer and composer, and a multimedia artist.

Christine Jette is a registered nurse and holds a Bachelor of Arts degree in psychology. She is the author of *Tarot Shadow Work* (2000), *Tarot for the Healing Heart, Tarot for All Seasons* (2001), and *Professional Tarot* (2003). Visit her on the web at: www.findingthemuse.com.

Corrine Kenner specializes in bringing metaphysical subjects down to earth. She is the author of two books on the tarot: *Tall, Dark Stranger*, a handbook on using tarot cards for romance, and *Tarot Journals*, a guide to the art of keeping a tarot diary. She is also the author of the *Epicurean Tarot*, the innovative recipe-card deck published by U.S. Games Systems, Inc., as well as Llewellyn's forthcoming *Crystals for Beginners*. A certified tarot master, she has studied tarot under the auspices of the Tarot School of New York, the Voyager Tarot Institute, and the Builders of the Adytum. Her own tarot classes and workshops are perennial favorites. Corrine

✷ ☆ ✷ ☆ ✷ ☆ ✷ ☆ ✷ ☆ ✷ ☆ ✷ ☆ ✷

lives in rural North Dakota with her husband Dan and her daughters Katherine, Emily, and Julia.

Edain McCoy has been in the Craft since 1981 and has been researching alternative spiritualities since her teens. Of greatest interest are Celtic, Appalachian, Curanderismo, Eclectic Wicca, Jewitchery, and Irish Witta. An alumna of the University of Texas with a B.A. in history, this former stockbroker now writes full-time and is affiliated with several professional writer's organizations. She is listed in the reference guides *Contemporary Authors*, *Who's Who Among American Women*, and *Who's Who In America*.

Mark McElroy is the author of *Putting the Tarot to Work*, a book on visual brainstorming for business, and *Taking the Tarot to Heart*, the brainstorming book for love, sex, and relationships.

Errol McLendon, CTI, is a tarot reader, writer, and teacher in the Chicago area where he lives with his wife, Wendye, and his dog-child, Morgan. Errol began reading cards in 1997 after a particularly unprofessional reading in New Orleans prompted him to buy his first deck to "find out what all this stuff is about." He continues to find out every day. As TarotGuy, Errol promotes tarot as "practical, not mystical." In addition to serving as the vice president of education for the American Tarot Association, Errol currently reads on two free-reading networks, regularly teaches a fifteen-week master class in Chicago, and mentors numerous students over the Internet.

Leeda Alleyn Pacotti practices as a naturopathic physician, nutritional counselor, and master herbalist, with occult studies and divination explorations spanning over forty years.

Rachel Pollack is the author of twenty-seven books of fiction and nonfiction, including two award-winning novels, and more than a dozen books on tarot. Her books include *The Kabbalah Tree*, *The Forest of Souls*, and *Seeker*, all published by Llewellyn. A visual artist as well as writer, she is the creator of *The Shining Tribe Tarot*, also available from Llewellyn.

Janina Renée is a scholar of material culture, folklore, mythology, ancient religion, psychology, medical anthropology, history, and literature. She is also the author of *Tarot Spells*, *Playful Magic*, *Tarot Your Everyday Guide*, *Tarot For a New Generation*, and *By Candlelight: Rites for Celebration, Blessing, and Prayer*.

Valerie Sim is the listowner of the popular tarot e-mail list "Comparative Tarot." Her first book, *Tarot Outside the Box*, was published in 2004, and she is now at work on her second book, *Shamanic Tarot*. She wrote the "little white book" for the recently published *Comparative Tarot Deck* and is the editor for both *Tarot Reflections* and the *ATA Quarterly*.

Thalassa is the producer of the San Francisco Bay Area Tarot Symposium (SF BATS), founder of Daughters of Divination (DOD), and publisher of *The Belfry* (purveyor of the finest divinatory journalism in the Western world). She reads, teaches, and produces divination-inspired events in both northern and southern California. She has been working with tarot, divination, and magic for more than thirty-six years, and wonders if she's ever going to see more than the shapely ankles of the Divine. She lives in San Francisco with a collection of swords, an assortment of historical costumes, too many books, and a tribe of semiferal dustbunnies—not to mention more tarot decks than one can safely shake a stick at.

James Wells is a Toronto-based tarot consultant, Reiki teacher, ritual weaver, and workshop facilitator. His aim is to assist people to reach their full potential. James has worked, played, and lived with the tarot since 1979 and thinks of the cards as his best friends and therapists. His creative, nonfatalistic, and sometimes irreverent style make him a popular consultant and teacher at home and abroad. Visit www.workeroforacles.com.

Diane Wilkes is a tarot author and teacher who has been reading cards for over thirty years. She is the author of the *Storyteller Tarot* and the forthcoming *Jane Austen Tarot*, which will be published by Lo Scarabeo in 2005. A certified tarot grand master, Diane is also the webmistress of Tarot Passages, a comprehensive and popular Internet site devoted primarily to tarot.

Winter Wren is a professional tarot reader and instructor from Central Illinois. She serves as president to the American Board for Tarot Certification. She is the author of a weekly tarot meditation available through her Tarot Box website. She spends her days reading, teaching, and writing about tarot at the Reborn Phoenix in Normal, Illinois.

The Fool

Tools for the Journey

Following the Fool

by Arnell Ando

This is a creative visualization that I like to read out loud when I do tarot-related art-therapy workshops. It helps get everyone a bit more relaxed, comfortable, and open to the gifts of the unconscious. I suggest they first find a relaxing position and take a few deep breaths before beginning, and I like to have some really lovely, unobtrusive music playing quietly in the background. I take my time by reading the visualization slowly, finding a rhythmic, hypnotic pace. I've gotten good feedback on this visualization and so I invite you to try it out the next time you have a gathering. Or if you prefer, you could read it to yourself on tape for a future encounter with the Fool.

Close your eyes now and relax. See if you can position yourself as comfortably as possible, shifting your weight so you're allowing your body to be fully supported.

Breathe deeply and slowly, and focus your attention on your breathing while you listen to the sound of my voice. As you breathe in, feel the life-giving air invigorating every part of you. As you breathe out, know that you are exhaling that which is used up and spent, while letting go of your tensions and weariness.

Breathing in . . . feel yourself filling with energy and light.

Breathing out . . . feel yourself giving up tension and resistance.

See yourself now on a remote beach. You face the water and behind you lies a sandy bank, a narrow grassy meadow and a deep, leafy forest. Imagine that you are standing up to your ankles in the warm ocean water. You feel the movement of the water and hear the cries of the seagulls overhead. Soft, fluffy clouds move slowly, lazily across the blue sky. A gentle breeze caresses your skin. The waves come in and cover your feet and then recede. As you inhale, the waves roll in . . . full of the energy of winds and tides as they softly massage your feet. As you exhale, the water recedes, washing away the tensions of your body. You remain there a while, breathing in and out with the movement of the ocean and being washed and caressed by the waves. You are becoming more and more peaceful and open, more centered with each breath, more and more deeply relaxed with each wave.

When you have reached the deep feeling of peace at your center, you turn and walk slowly from the water toward the grassy, leafy forest at the edge of the sand. You see what looks to be a very old path leading into the woods. The shady forest beckons you. The grass is grown over in parts, but still the path is visible. Slowly, serenely, you begin to follow the path into the grove. Soon you are deep among the trees, walking in cool shade, hearing the rustling of

the leaves and the chirping of birds, inhaling the smells of the leafy canopy and the rich soil of the forest floor. The trees are getting bigger as you walk along. Their trunks are gnarled and covered in plush, green moss. The path is soft beneath your feet.

You hear the faint sound of tinkling bells and soft laughter. You look around and see no one . . . but you faintly hear someone humming a playful tune—something old . . . familiar, yet not quite recognizable. It reminds you of a distant memory of childhood. If you could just remember the words you could return to that exact memory . . . but the words are just beyond your grasp.

Suddenly a brightly colored fellow jumps playfully in front of you, spinning cartwheels, going head over heels for your amusement. He has bells on his curly yellow shoes and wears more tinkling bells on the sloping, pointy hat of a court jester. He winks mischievously and disappears into the glade. You look around and see a spotted dog watching the place where your new friend must be hiding, and so you move slowly towards the dog. The dog cocks her head and gives you the once-over, but you pass inspection and she leads you to the Fool. You find him sitting on a flat rock, playing with a deck of cards. As you get closer you notice that the images on the cards are shifting. As he shuffles the cards you see memories of your lifetime—and beyond—flash before you. A family gathering, a secret pact with friends, a trip to the lake, a birthday celebration . . . and then more images, hazy and unfocused so that you can't quite place them, though you recognize yourself and some of the characters.

The Fool stops shuffling and begins to put the cards in a pattern on the flat rock. Again you see yourself and recognize some of the people and settings in the cards . . . but others seem foreign to you, as if they have not yet taken place. The pattern seems to be mapping out a story, an adventure with you as the hero. Adrenaline rushes up your spine as you realize how exciting this all is. You move closer, catching the attention of your new friend. You ask if you may trade for this magical deck of cards. He gives you a sly smile and asks what you have to give in exchange. You feel around in the pockets of your faded jeans and pull out the objects within: an old Zippo lighter, a folding tin cup, a penknife, and a lucky rock you once favored. You are surprised to see these treasures because you thought you had lost them long ago. These were all important to you once, and you are filled with a feeling of warm nostalgia at seeing them again. But what must you give up in order to obtain this magical deck of cards? The Fool tells you these tokens still serve you well and that they represent the four elements of fire, water, air, and earth, but—"Haven't you got something else you are really ready to part with?" You check your shirt pocket (the one that rests above your heart) and you pull out a faded photo. A memory tinged with sadness crosses your mind. Can you make out the faded image in the picture?

He asks to see it, and as you hand it to him, a burden lifts from your shoulders . . . a weight that you didn't notice was there until it was lifted. He smiles, nods, and says, "Yes, this will be a fair trade. Letting go of something worn out, that no longer serves you, for this new companion and guide." He smiles wisely and you realize you know this familiar, gentle face. He has been a friend under different guises at different times in your life and will continue to be so. He wraps the deck of cards in a black silk handkerchief and hands them to you. You thank him, and he smiles and wishes you well on your journey.

You hold on to the cards tightly as you walk the path out of the woods. You feel excited about the future and the journey you are on. You feel a sense of purpose and a surge of energy and bright optimism that feels as warm and inviting as the Sun peeking through the trees. As you draw closer to the edge of the forest, you look back once and hear the soft chanting of a childhood melody and a dog howling in the far distance. You feel certain you could find this place again whenever you have a desire to visit. You walk the path that leads out of the woods, aware of the light getting brighter and brighter with each step that you take. Notice now the aliveness, the eagerness and energy that you feel.

And so . . . feel yourself slowly returning to this room, breathing in and out . . . very rhythmically and easily, gently and with soft eyes, coming back into this reality whenever you are ready.

One-Card Readings

by Elizabeth Genco

At the beginning of your tarot studies, you may get the impression that lots of cards and complications are the norm (or even required) in readings. No matter what deck you have, you can be fairly certain that the instructional materials that came with it contain at the very least that old chestnut of spreads, the Celtic Cross. Spreads of eight or more cards are liberally sprinkled throughout the tarot lexicon; such spreads certainly give you a very thorough picture of a situation. But there can be such a thing as too much information. What's more, there's a fine line between complex and superfluous (not to mention confusing) when it comes to tarot.

Next time you're confronted with a sticky issue and want to consult the cards, why not try a one-card reading? Such readings give you a discrete focus; they get to the heart of a situation right away. A one-card reading is perfect if you want to skip the possible distraction of looking at things from all sides—for those times when you "just want an answer."

Don't be fooled into thinking that one-card readings are just for mundane issues. With the tarot's richness in symbolism (even on most pip cards), droves of good advice and meaning can be found on a single card, even for "the big stuff." Each of tarot's seventy-eight cards contain layers of meaning. One-card readings on a very specific issue can draw these different layers to the surface. The card may seem completely random at first glance, especially if you have no supporting cards to draw on. But with a little thought, new interpretations will arise, providing you with information not only for your current problem but for future readings as well.

If nothing else, one-card readings can act as a fresh, "no holds barred" pair of eyes on a situation. Think of a one-card reading as your wise old aunt offering up advice: she's got no shortage of opinions, and she won't hesitate to cut to the quick and tell you exactly what you need to hear in the fewest possible words. Below are a few ways to make the one-card reading work for you.

1) Here's something that you probably haven't tried in a long time: the purely intuitive reading. Now, before you jump to the conclusion that such a suggestion is heresy for a tarot reader ("What? Cast aside all that knowledge that I've spent months/years learning in favor of listening to myself?!"), remember that there was a time that you didn't know anything about tarot, and, in some ways, you had as much knowledge then as you do now. Also, your intuition comes into play in every reading to at least some degree, regardless of how much "book learnin'" you've put into the tarot. The cards of some decks were designed with intuition in mind (the *Rider-Waite-Smith*, the model for the majority of decks on the market today, is a good example). Besides, your tarot skills won't go away. In fact, if you've spent that much time learning tarot, a good deal of your knowledge will be internalized and just might show up in a reading anyway.

A one-card reading is the perfect place to break free of tarot tradition and let the images on the card simply speak to you. You may find that they have a lot more to do with your problem than you would have expected. And, when you're willing to sit quietly and listen to yourself, you may find that your intuition has a lot more to say about it, too.

2) On the subject of intuitive readings, here's a simple, effective technique from Wald and Ruth Ann Amberstone of the Tarot School in New York City. When interpreting your card, find one symbol in the image that reaches out to you, and then read only that symbol. This is a great way to develop your intuitive skills (though it's certainly possible that your interpretation of a particular symbol will

be based on your learned meaning of that symbol, and that's okay). Interpreting a single symbol on the entire card will direct your focus to a very specific point, which may be exactly what you need for the issue at hand.

3) Create a "spread" for the problem, but make it a one-card spread. As with all spreads, the sky's the limit in deciding what that card will represent. A few possibilities:

- the root of the situation
- the main obstacle
- the unknown
- the unconscious
- the environment
- the outcome
- your greatest ally
- the one thing that you need to focus on

Even the most complicated situations oftentimes have straightforward, uncomplicated issues at their roots. A one-card spread strips down the question to its single most important aspect.

4) Another possibility for a one-card reading is to use that one card to get a specific, concrete course of action, or a next step that you can take. Turning to the cards for advice on what action to take is an often-overlooked but very important part of tarot practice. Many beginning readers (and querents!) get so hung up on the idea that

tarot will tell them what is going to happen that they forget the bigger issue of, "Well, given that I know that, what do I do now?" Consulting the tarot on what "concrete steps" (to quote the wonderful Nina Lee Braden) you can take to solve your problem is empowering, not to mention the fact that it'll go a lot farther toward getting the problem resolved, which is probably what you want to do in the first place.

Frame your question in terms of what you need to do next, then select one card. With no room for small talk, you'll get right to the heart of the matter and learn what to do next. With this practice, you are once again focusing on direct access to your question's core issue.

5) To make your one-card readings even more specific, you can add a time limit to it. Ask the cards about a "concrete step" or a "most important thing" to focus on within a certain time. Whether you're reading one or many cards, time limits frame the question and are a good tarot practice. For a one-card reading, they add even more direction and focus. With a one-card reading, a reasonable time frame, such as one week to three months, is usually best.

Lastly, in addition to all the techniques outlined above, there is nothing wrong with playing it straight: asking your question, drawing a single card for your answer, and interpreting that card as you ordinarily would. You haven't spent all that time learning those card meanings for nothing! You also might find it useful to combine two or all of the last three techniques. For example, perform a one-card spread, then select another card for the next concrete step, adding a time limit to one or the other card.

When you've got seventy-eight cards packed with meaning, it's easy to get bogged down. Don't be afraid to simplify your practice. When you're looking for a no-frills approach, a one-card reading may be your best bet. It's a great way to get a clear, direct answer to a question, or the most straightforward advice as to what to do next.

The Voice in the Card

by Ruth Ann and Wald Amberstone

One of the most powerful and versatile techniques we teach at the Tarot School is an intuitive reading method we call the Voice in the Card. It works with any deck and can be used effectively by novices and professionals alike. It's simple to explain but can be very subtle, as you'll see.

Hearing the Voice

Choose a card by any method you like. Next, take some time to study the picture very carefully. Look at everything. What is the landscape made of? What is the sky or background like? Are there any people in the card? If so, pay attention to their clothing, posture, facial expression, hair color, jewelry, etc. What are the predominant colors in the card? What kind of buildings are there, if any?

Once you've had a chance to observe the card as a whole, allow your eyes to focus on a single detail or aspect of the card—the one that stands out the most. It's likely that a number of different items will vie for your attention at first, but eventually you'll find yourself coming back to one detail more often than the others. The voice in the card speaks through that image or detail. It can tell you something that the person receiving the reading needs to know, something particularly interesting or insightful about him or her, or something he or she should do.

This is strictly an intuitive reading and the message you receive from your chosen symbol will have nothing to do with the "meaning" of the card. This is why the technique can be used by someone who has no prior knowledge of tarot. If you're an experienced reader, you can easily use it with a deck you've never seen before. The trick in either case is to quiet the mind enough to allow the message to come through. Don't censor yourself. This is the place where you can take risks with your interpretation and possibly "amaze your friends!"

Sometimes the message will be a simple and obvious one. For instance, if you pull the Sun and your attention is drawn to the picture of the Sun or the words "The Sun" printed on the card, the message might be that you (or your querent) need to get out in the Sun a little more. Or perhaps Sunday is an important day for some reason. Other times, the reading can lead to contemplation and a deeper meaning of great significance can emerge. In this case, the Sun may have a psychological or even spiritual message.

The best way to demonstrate the technique and value of the voice in the card is through example. The following are actual readings from three Tarot School correspondence course students. These exercises were submitted as part of their coursework and they have graciously offered to share them with you.

Anna

Taking the *Universal Waite Tarot* deck in my hand, I walked into the living room and put on some relaxing music. Moving in front of my favorite chair, I cast my Circle of Time (another exercise in the course) and then sat down. With my front door open to the warm sunny morning and listening to the birds singing, I inhaled deeply and then exhaled. I did this for a few moments and let my breathing return to normal. I could feel a pleasant atmosphere and heard the soothing soft music in the background. I picked up the phone and called my friend, Karyn.

After sitting down and quieting my thoughts, I became aware of how pleasant the morning was. I could hear birds singing and calling to each other outside, and the music was light and airy. It was so relaxing and I had the sense that this was going to be a good reading for my friend. I don't know why—just something I felt inside. I got a kind of excited feeling when dialing the phone and just knew she would get a great message and it would be very helpful to her.

I find that the card drawn has a voice in the card for whomever that particular card is for. Something in it will jump out at me, move, or speak to me in some way, and inevitably it will be for that person. The only thing is that it doesn't seem to come very quickly. Although I wish it would, it doesn't. I also start to get impressions, and these often lead into something else, and so I have learned to start talking. I say what I hear, see, smell, touch, and speak about them. I get impressions in pictures that seem to be symbolic, and I sometimes need to interpret them. What it may mean to me isn't always what it means to the person I am doing this exercise for. If I don't understand what I am seeing or sensing then I always ask the person if that means anything to them. So I have learned to interact with the person.

After talking for a little bit, she and I did the exercise and the card drawn was the Knight of Cups. I scanned the image on this card from the bottom to the top. My eye at first caught the water running across the card. I said that the water is considered to be the River of Life and emotions. I saw it moving and could also hear it. It wasn't real loud, but noticeable. I could see the horse wanting to take a step, yet hesitating. It seemed like it was confused about a decision—whether to take that step and cross the water and move into unknown territory or to stay by the water. Scanning up the card slowly, my eyes fell on the horse's mane and its wavelike shape. My vision then fell onto the winged helmet and centered in on the wings. I started to see the wings flap back and forth, just like a bird's.

I told her that my focus was on the wings on the Knight's helmet. She said, "Oh my!" I then got the sense of flying and soaring. I told her, "I feel like I am flying and soaring like a bird. First the flapping of the wings and then the sense of flying and soaring, even floating." I then heard the birds singing outside and also envisioned a bird. This bird I saw was a most beautiful bird, very colorful, happy, singing, flapping its wings, swinging on a swing, running back and forth in a cage. I said to her, "I am not sure why I see this, but I see a very beautiful, colorful bird, and it is very happy and ecstatic, in a cage. It looks like a parakeet or parrot of some kind."

She gasped and said, "I've been wondering if I should get a bird lately. My cat has recently died and I have been wanting a bird, but I didn't know whether I should get one or not."

I answered, "Get one! This card is telling you to get one."

She told me she has been very lonely since her cat passed on, but she didn't want another cat. She was honestly thinking about getting a bird.

She got the bird right away, and it's a parakeet. She said it is a very colorful male bird and she hopes to teach it to talk soon. She named him "Knighty" because of the tarot reading. She does seem like she is enjoying the companionship and is starting to train him to get on her finger. Isn't that fun? She shared with me later that she took the Voice in the Card reading as her green light to go ahead. I said that the desert landscape across the water was probably what she was feeling after her cat went to heaven, and it was looking pretty desolate until Knighty. She laughed and said that she already loves him and thanked me for the fun reading.

It is so much fun and rewarding when I can help someone like my friend. She shared with me recently how much she loves her parakeet. I am so glad she took my Voice in the Card reading to heart. If she didn't she would probably still be very lonely.

Carmen

I did this exercise on a Sunday morning. I was very relaxed after a big breakfast. My husband was upstairs reading. I was downstairs in the room that we call the computer room. My dog was sleeping at my feet. It was very quiet in my neighborhood. I had the window open, and it was pleasantly cool. I shuffled my cards on top of the futon in that room. I like to spread the cards on a large surface, then mix the cards thoroughly. I was thinking about what I should consider now in my life. I stacked the cards, cut them in three groups, and from the right-hand pile I drew the Seven of Pentacles.

I looked at the card, I stared at the card, I scanned every detail in the card. I looked at the farmer's tool, then I looked at his clothes, then at the background, and the leaves. Nothing came to me. Finally, after a long while, I saw the big pile of leaves and pentacles and nothing else.

I saw the high pile of leaves and pentacles as lots of stuff, and that brought me to see my own stuff—my tangible and intangible things. Then I started my reasoning process. I began to see all the knowledge and experience that I had accumulated throughout my life. I felt that it was time to consider what my assets are and where I stand in life. It is time to consider what I have achieved and acquired, and decide whether or not I want to use what I have or if I prefer

to steer in a different direction and start again. This card came to me because I have been thinking about changing my line of work.

I had achieved so much, but in the process I had killed myself a lot, too. There is a fine line where fun and success stop and they become trial and drudgery. For that reason, I want to change my career to something less stressful, something where I can enjoy the good things that life offers, like sunrises and sunsets. I want to be able to leave my house when it is daylight and come back when it is still light, too. I want to dedicate myself more to my home, and put an end to my daily three-hour commute.

I see in the pile of leaves that I may have enough financial resources to downsize myself. I have to be a careful planner, start counting my pentacles, and separate my pentacles from my leaves—create different piles and start organizing. Perhaps the solution is to work at a place near my home.

I am willing to count my strengths and my weaknesses, and stop this social charade. I am the only one who loses. I come from a society where one does not put in the trash anything that is not completely destroyed. Here I am buying stuff and tossing it away like it did not cost me hours of hard work and aggravation. I have accumulated so much stuff. I honestly do not need anything else. I started doing a mental search, and reached the conclusion that the garage is full of good stuff and junk that for some reason I do not use. I have stuff galore. Why do I keep that stuff if I do not use it?

The pile of leaves and pentacles in this card told me that I had accumulated material junk. I need to declutter my house of old things, and the same pile of leaves and pentacles also told me that

I can apply the same decluttering towards my life. I can live a simple life without having to accumulate things. Why then accumulate more? When I say accumulate things I mean to declutter my heart from false pretensions and get rid of old ways of thinking.

While I was working on this exercise I felt a great relief. I have not yet planned where I should go searching for a new job. I may have to obtain a new set of skills. I am still uncertain about how to work out the details, but I am pretty sure that after some thinking I will be able to sort out an answer. Writing down my fears of doing something different opened a new door for me. It was open before, but I could not see it.

Definitely, I learned that I am still bound to what other people think about me. I thought while doing this exercise about the possibility of working for a nonglamorous place where I could run into acquaintances or friends, and honestly it gave me the creeps. I must work to overcome that attitude. That attitude is vicious; I was not aware that I had that train of thought so buried in my heart.

Thanks to this exercise, I am discovering the dark face of myself. Spooky! I never saw myself tied to society that badly. I felt good throughout the exercise, and I had a feeling of well-being. I was moved by the contrast in the colors of the leaves and the pentacles. My train of thought flowed easily from one idea to another. After performing this exercise, I can truly say that I learned about myself. I am not who I thought I was; I am still a prisoner of society's approval.

Timothy

I shuffled the cards and let them sit for twenty-four hours. The next day, I spread them out on a table in front of my girlfriend, Kristen. She selected the card that, as she said, "gave off the most heat." Kristen drew the Queen of Pentacles.

As I looked at it, the first detail that caught my attention was the rabbit, which immediately reminded me of Kristen's rabbit, Kera. But I wasn't sure this was what the message was supposed to be about, so I kept searching the card for something else. Eventually, I realized that my gaze kept locking onto the rabbit, so I decided to concentrate on that image. I thought of a rabbit running across the street and I asked Kristen if she had almost hit a bunny lately while driving. She said no. She said she had seen a wild, baby bunny sitting in the grass outside our house, however. But I didn't know what to do with this information, so I decided to just keep concentrating on the rabbit in the picture. At this point, I made a very conscious effort to listen to the rabbit in the card while trying not to project my own thoughts and expectations onto it.

Very shortly after, I heard a voice say: "I need food!" I told Kristen this and she went to check on Kera's food dish. Oddly enough, it was empty. Afterwards, Kristen said she thought she remembered filling it earlier that day, so she was surprised to find it empty.

Every time I do the Voice in the Card reading, I feel like I get a little better at remaining open to whatever impressions or sensations will come. This time I learned that remaining open is a lot like trying to silence the inner noise during meditation. And just like in meditation, counting breaths, or at least just focusing on the process of breathing, is very helpful.

I believe this reading met the three criteria of a good reading as specified in the course: it was surprising, useful, and true.

Applications

Once you have become comfortable with the Voice in the Card as a one-card reading, you'll discover how versatile the technique is by incorporating it into larger spreads. Decide silently before laying out a spread which position in a spread you will use for a Voice in the Card reading, in addition to its usual interpretation. This will give an added psychic layer and a much-appreciated nuance to the reading as a whole.

Here are three ways to use the Voice in the Card in a larger reading:

1) If a card turns up in a reading that doesn't immediately suggest anything useful, you may find yourself momentarily blocked. What to do? The Voice in the Card method is an excellent way to derive useful information from this card and keep the reading moving.

2) Sometimes you'll have a querent you'd like to involve more deeply in the reading process. Ask the querent to pick a detail in the card and look within for its message. This tends to nicely boost the give-and-take of an otherwise one-sided conversation.

3) The Voice in the Card reading can be highly proactive. With this technique, any card in a spread can become what we call a "Magician's Wand." Simply by the reader's intent, the detail in the Voice in the Card reading will give its message in the form of an action the querent can take to bring about a result. This may be the first step in a course of action leading to a desired outcome.

If you come to enjoy this technique, you will find your own uses for it. It just gets better and better, more and more useful with practice, even if you feel that your psychic ability isn't strong to begin with. The more often you do it, the more you'll please and surprise your querents, and what may be even better, the more you'll please and surprise yourself!

Seventy-Eight Faces of Divinity

by Nina Lee Braden

For a long time, tarot has been my primary spiritual tool. But recently, I discovered that, for me, tarot was more than a spiritual tool. In fact, the faces of the tarot cards themselves could be seen as seventy-eight different faces of divinity. Although this realization was relatively sudden, its development was not. I think that my first glimpse of this concept of tarot as a mirror of the divine was when I was a member of *APA Tarot*. *APA Tarot* predated the Internet and was a monthly publication of individual "'zines'" or newsletters which were bundled together into one issue. Tarot collector and expert Frank Jensen was a member of *APA Tarot*, and one of his interests was in "Pixie's faces." Frank would crop and enlarge faces from the *Rider-Waite-Smith Tarot*. Usually, these faces were black-and-white line drawings only, but sometimes Frank would print them in blue and white or red and white. The effects were startling and insightful, and I developed a new appreciation for the artistic talent of Pamela "Pixie" Colman Smith. I began looking at and pondering the faces on the cards. A seed of interest had been planted.

Later, I was pondering a possible tarot workshop idea to teach at a Unitarian Universalist church. By this time, I was using tarot as a spiritual tool, and I conceived the idea of teaching the tarot's Major

Arcana as twenty-two gateways to divinity. I also planned to show in this workshop that humanity and divinity were mirrors of each other (having by this time been introduced to the Hermetic axiom of "as above, so below"). The Unitarian Universalists decided not to take me up on my workshop offer, but the idea of tarot as a gateway to divinity continued to grow in my mind.

Let me make clear that when I speak of the tarot as faces of the divine, I do not mean that I worship or pray to the cards themselves. Instead, I see the energies, figures, or archetypes behind the physical cards as symbols of the divine. The cards themselves are just pieces of paper, but they also are physical representations of divine energy and can be powerful catalysts for our personal spiritual work. As physical representations of divine energy, the tarot can help us to focus our prayers, meditations, and rituals for greatest effect. When we pray to the Great Mother facet of divine energy, we can mentally picture the Empress. When we meditate on hope as an expression of the divine, we can mentally picture the Star. The tarot can become not only an abstract or theoretical expression of divine energy but also a practical spiritual tool.

Many people use the twenty-two cards of the Major Arcana to represent different attributes or aspects of the divine. After all, it is fairly easy to see the divine in the Empress, the Star, and the Sun. We

can even encompass a view of the divine that allows for the Tower, the Devil, and Death. But many of us overlook the fifty-six cards of the Minor Arcana as windows into the divine, and this is a mistake.

At first, like many other tarot teachers, I focused primarily on the Major Arcana, giving only cursory attention to the Minor Arcana. Although much has been written on the Major Arcana as a spiritual tool, there hasn't been a lot of similar work done on the Minor Arcana. However, the more that I continued to work with the cards, the more I came to see that the whole deck had spiritual value, and I gradually came to see all seventy-eight cards as faces both of humanity and divinity. Each card shows a unique face of the divine and a unique face of humanity, and study of the cards is a way to better know the divine and to know humanity. Without books, with only careful attention to study and meditation upon the pictures and symbols of the cards, one could learn volumes about divinity and humanity.

Quickly, let me note that I do not advise throwing away all of your tarot books. I am a firm believer in studying. I am only saying that without reading books, one can still learn a great deal about divinity and humanity from the visual images of the cards. If you add the wisdom that others have recorded in books to your own visual study, you truly have access to the wisdom of the ages.

Let us more closely consider the images, the faces, of the tarot. We have men and women, sages and children, kings and paupers. From this we can surmise that humanity is male and female, old and young, and rich and poor. Indeed, it takes very little wisdom to agree with this premise. However, let us also look at the divine in these terms. Can we accept the divine as male and female? Old and young? Rich and poor? Upon thought and reflection, most of us can. In addition, the divine is both comforting and awe-inspiring, and likewise, so are the images on the tarot cards. So in my spiritual belief system, I began to see that God has seventy-eight faces. As I work with the tarot, each face teaches me and challenges me to the extent that I allow it.

How many of us have felt the divine in a rainbow, a raindrop, a leaf, or a breeze? When we stop and observe, we realize that the divine is all around us. Each hug, each smile, and each tear is a manifestation of the divine. It therefore becomes simple to also see the divine in the cards of the Minor Arcana as well. The Six of Cups reflects divinity in the giving of simple gifts. The Three of Swords reveals divinity in the expression of honest grief. The Two of

Pentacles shows us divinity in juggling our daily tasks. The Four of Wands illustrates the divinity of public celebration.

If we only pause, we can easily see the divine in each of the seventy-eight cards of the tarot. One of my favorite activities is to simply look at a tarot deck, faceup. I will look at each card for a second or a few seconds, and then go on to the next card. At the end of my perusal of the cards, I feel renewed, reassured, and refreshed. I feel as if I have been in communion with the divine, and, indeed, I have. Sometimes, as I look through the cards, I will stop on a particular card. Something about the face of a character on a card will strike my attention, or perhaps a previously unremarked symbol will "shout" to me, "Look! Notice me! I'm important." The physical tarot deck becomes a vehicle for divine communication.

Although each face of the divine is holy and has a message for me, on different days different faces will speak to me more easily or more urgently. One of the advantages of familiarity with the tarot is that I don't have to have a physical deck of cards with me to connect with the faces. If I am afraid or nervous, I can mentally picture the serene face of the High Priestess and I can "talk" with her. I do not need a deck of cards present, only my mental image of the card. If I also need some boldness, after I have calmed down I might picture the Knight of Swords charging to the rescue. I might draw on the Knight's drive and focus to help me in my own task.

Once we have determined that each tarot card illustrates a face of the divine, it is easy to think of the tarot as seventy-eight faces of divinity. If we think of ourselves as reflections of divinity, it is easy to think of the tarot also as depicting seventy-eight faces of humanity. When we think of the divine, it is a mistake to limit ourselves to only a few concepts. If I see the divine as revealed only by a few cards of the tarot, I am limiting the power of divinity in my life. Likewise, if I only use a few cards to see myself (and others), then I am limiting my own potential and the potential of others. tarot is an effective bridge, conveying the message that to be divine is to be human and to be human is to be divine, not only "as above, so below," but also "as below, so above."

This dual portraiture of tarot, picturing divinity and humanity simultaneously, helps to remind me of the divinity of my daily life. Doing laundry is not drudgery, but a spiritual exercise; I am the Star, pouring cleansing water over the land. Driving to work, I am the Chariot, channeling the divine will through concentration and focus. Sometimes the spiritual connections are not as easy to see, but they are there. On some days I reflect the Queen of Pentacles—busily managing my affairs and delegating and overseeing tasks. On other days, I am the figure in the Eight of Pentacles—an apprentice, learning a new task. Still other days, I am the person in the Seven of Cups—full of dreams and imagination. I am human; I am divine; and tarot shows that humanity and divinity are one.

I frequently use affirmations as a practical application of the tarot's bridge between divinity and humanity. A good daily affirmation to remind ourselves of tarot's reflection of divinity and humanity might be: "I recognize the divine in every person. I recognize the divine in myself. I recognize the divine in nature. I recognize the divine in all. All is divine, and the tarot is the reflection of all."

On the following page is a series of twenty-two affirmations on love, based on the Major Arcana. These affirmations could easily be extended throughout the rest of the Minor Arcana.

Major Arcana Affirmations

Fool: I love foolishly, impetuously, boldly, and instinctively.

Magician: I love with attention.

High Priestess: I love wisely, from within my subconscious.

Empress: I love sensually and creatively.

Emperor: I love logically and with clear vision.

Hierophant: I teach love and establish traditions of love.

Lovers: I love with discrimination and discernment.

Chariot: I will to love.

Strength: I love both passionately and gently.

Hermit: I stretch out my hand in love.

Wheel of Fortune: I love in riches or poverty, sickness or health.

Justice: I love harmoniously, bringing balance through love.

Hanged Man: I make willing sacrifices for love.

Death: I love transformatively.

Temperance: I test and temper my love.

Devil: I love joyfully, with mirth.

Tower: I powerfully awaken to love, beginning anew each day.

Star: I love hopefully and peacefully.

Moon: I love reflectively and even as I sleep.

Sun: I love radiantly and shine my love through my face.

Judgement: I love decisively; I love with a bite.

World: I dance with the love to the rhythm of all.

Tarot for Two

by Mark McElroy

I f you've been with your husband, wife, spouse, partner, significant other—you know, that person you call Love Monkey or Sugar Britches or Hot Lips—for any length of time, chances are good that you've fallen into a comfortable routine.

Ah, the comforts of routine. Who cooks breakfast? Who gets the paper? Who dresses fastest? Who heads off to work first? How often do you touch base during the day? When do you get home in the evenings? How do you handle dinner? Are your evenings spent working out together? Watching television? Reading each other seventeenth-century German love poems while soaking in a hot tub full of lime Jello? (If you haven't tried that last bit, you don't know what you're missing.)

My point is this: humans are essentially creatures of habit. Once partnered, a routine evolves within a matter of weeks. Once it's in place, we can turn a significant chunk of our daily planning over to our built-in AutoPilot. It's convenient. It's comforting. It's probably even healthy.

But please note the word I use to describe how routines come to be: they evolve. In most cases, there little or no intention involved. We don't set out to wind up in front of the television watching *Big Brother 15* every Wednesday at 8:30 . . . we just wind up there. How much of your routine as a couple is dictated by chance . . . by work . . . or by circumstance? How much of it is a matter of choice or intention?

With time—often before we realize it—our routine reduces the profound magic of being together into something, well, *routine*. We don't intend to quit surprising each other with flowers . . . we just do. We don't intend to stop drawing our partners a candlelit bath . . . we just do. We don't intend to stop making time to talk about who we are and where we're going as a couple . . . we just do. Suddenly, before we realize it, we're taking each other for granted.

Tarot for Two is a fast, fun, friendly game you can use to shatter routine and restore a sense of playful awareness in your relationship. Much of this game's powerful magic is rooted in the evocative images that appear on every card and their ability to quickly communicate complex messages.

A big part of its power, though, is also rooted in your own intention. When you and your partner schedule time to play this game together, you're making a conscious choice to invest time in enhancing and exploring your relationship. Instead of allowing your partnership to drift along like a leaf in a river, you're communicating, collaborating, and charting your own course!

What You'll Need

The tarot. Obviously, you'll need a deck of tarot cards (this isn't the 2006 *I Ching Reader*, after all). I suggest (much to the delight of deck publishers like Llewellyn) that you each have a deck of your own.

Your decks don't have to be exactly alike, so this will be a good chance for obsessive collectors to demonstrate to their partners why you *really do* need more than one deck. Using different decks also provides unique opportunities for insight. Let's say you choose to represent your partner's best quality with the *World Spirit* Strength card. Your partner might also choose to represent her own best quality with a Strength card . . . but if hers is the equivalent card from *Medieval Enchantment*, the *Gilded Tarot*, or the *Bright Idea Deck*, she probably chose it for different reasons. Comparing and contrasting the two cards can yield fascinating new perspectives.

If your decks are just alike (remember that duplicate copy of the *World Spirit* deck you picked up for free at that last tarot conference?), you can experience the thrill of both having answered the same question with identical cards. Turning over cards that match exactly is pretty dramatic; celebrate the moment with high fives, warm embraces, or a congratulatory sip of wine. (If, after several congratulatory sips of wine, your partner becomes more interested in you than the cards . . . well, even if you never finish the game, you both win.)

Incidentally, while some knowledge of the tarot can be helpful, neither you nor your partner has to know a thing about tarot in order to play.

At least an hour of uninterrupted time. Don't even think about trying to squeeze this game in between commercial breaks. Sure, you can use your Palm Pilot to schedule "Achieve Intimacy" into a thirty-minute block of time . . . but how realistic is that? And what's the rush? The whole point of the exercise is to slow down and spend time with each other.

A place to play. You can play this game anywhere . . . but you'll get more out of it if you'll get in the mood. Set the stage a bit. Light some candles. Put on some jazzy music. Put out a plate or two of your favorite snacks.

And for heaven's sake, turn off televisions, pagers, computers, and cell phones, all of which produce anti-romantic radiation. (Anti-romantic radiation is no laughing matter, folks. If you don't believe in it, remove all televisions, pagers, computers, and telephones from your bedroom for a week. The results will surprise you—and you'll thank me later on!)

A notepad and pen. As you play, you're very likely to want to jot some things down. Not a note taker? Keep that pen and paper handy anyway—you might be inspired to whip up an impromptu Valentine greeting during a break.

Special Tips to Enhance Your Pleasure

Relax. Despite the section header above, this game doesn't call for the use of specialty condoms. (You might have some on hand, though, just in case.) Instead, it offers a few suggestions designed to help you get the most out of every game. Remember:

It's not rugby. Our competitive world turns some people into fierce competitors; tonight's game, however, is one of cooperation, not competition. Tarot for Two is not a full-contact sport. You aren't trying to prove your superiority here. Running around the table screaming, "I win! I win! I winnnnnn!" is frowned upon.

Keep it light. Tarot for Two isn't a substitute for couples therapy. If suppressed aggression or unspoken resentment are eating away at your relationship, more expedient ways exist for dealing with those issues. This game isn't an invitation to nitpick; it's a chance to celebrate what's going right.

Red is a romantic color, unless we're talking about ink. Resist any urges to edit, modify, mark up, or revise your partner's choices and comments. Remember: you're here to listen, learn, and love . . . not grade your partner's work. Whatever your partner chooses and whatever logic he or she uses to justify that choice is The Right Answer, period.

How to Play

Tarot for Two is a card game consisting of four distinct rounds, designed to be played in order: Personal Portraits, The All-Seeing I, Surprise/Surprise, and Going Places.

Round One: Personal Portraits

Without revealing your choices to each other, go through your tarot deck and choose two cards: one to represent you and one to represent your partner. Place the card that represents you facedown on your left; place the card representing your partner facedown on your right.

You may choose these cards for any reason. The card may represent an attitude, an action, an emotion, or a personality trait you associate with your partner. Maybe the card is associated with the astrological sign for Cancer, and your partner was born on July 10. Maybe the guy on the Page of Cups has a haircut just like yours. The logic you use doesn't matter—but you should be able to explain the reasons that led you to your choice.

When both of you have locked in your selections, reveal them . . . and the logic you used when selecting the card. What choices did you make? What relationships exist between the cards? You can explore the cards in any number of ways: by adding up their values for a numerological comparison, by referencing their astrological associations, by looking for a pattern in suits or elements or colors, or even by comparing the postures and expressions of the people on the cards themselves.

Round Two: The All-Seeing I

Collect all the cards, shuffle them, and draw three cards at random. Place these facedown on the table in a straight line from left to right. Without revealing them to your partner, take a look at each card.

Card 1, on the far left, represents "What I've learned from this relationship." How have you grown as a result of being with your partner? What improvements have you made? What insights have you achieved? What have you achieved with your partner that you wouldn't have achieved alone?

Card 2, in the middle, represents "What I bring to the relationship." What gifts do you contribute? What strengths do you provide? Let this card inspire you to consider whatever it is that you do best, and how it makes being together easier and more fun than being apart.

Card 3, on the far right, represents "What I can do to improve our relationship." Even if most every day you're together is like a rerun of *The Donna Reed Show*, every relationship can grow. Is there an action you can take on your own or your partner's behalf? A chore you can assume? An attitude you can adjust? A forgiveness you can extend? A prejudice you can cast aside? A toilet seat you can remember to put down on a regular basis? What can you personally do to help take your relationship to the next level?

Once you've established these answers for yourself, make some notes . . . and then, switch sides. Now you're looking at the cards that describe your partner's growth, your partner's special gift to the relationship, and a suggestion for something your partner can do to improve the relationship. With your partner in mind, come up with your own interpretations for the very same cards.

When you're done, compare your interpretations. Remember to take your partner's statements at face value—no editing or correcting! (Demonstrations of affection, however, are strongly encouraged.)

Round Three: Surprise/Surprise

Return all cards to the deck and shuffle thoroughly. Draw three additional cards, again placing them facedown in a straight line.

> Card 1 represents an idea for a romantic weekend.
>
> Card 2 represents an idea for an inexpensive gift costing less than $9.95 (hmmm . . . about the price of a new tarot deck!).
>
> Card 3 represents a spicy little idea to try in the bedroom (or wherever your passions take you!).

Without revealing your cards to your partner, take a look at each one. Allow yourself just sixty seconds per card, and jot down every single idea that pops into your head, no matter how ridiculous, silly, or inane. The idea is to get down as many answers as possible in the least amount of time. (Even ideas you discard as impractical or too expensive—like, say, a trip to the Grand Canyon—might later prompt an idea you *can* afford—like buying a travel book and planning a dream trip that the two of you can start saving money for.)

When time is up, don't share your lists! Instead, count your total number of answers. The person who came up with the most ideas gets a passionate kiss, and the person who came up with the least ideas gets to kiss back.

Finally, later this week, you must make one of the ideas that occurred to you in this round into a reality. Take that trip, surprise your partner with that gift, or try something new in the boudoir. The only way to lose this round is to refuse to play!

Round Four: Going Places

Return all cards to the deck. If you're working with two decks, use only one deck for this round. Shuffle the deck well and draw three final cards, placing them facedown in a straight line, as before.

> Card 1 represents "What we want to achieve together."
>
> Card 2 represents "A strategy for growing closer."

Card 3 represents "A wish for our future."

Interpret these cards together, suggesting as many ideas as you can for each card. Agreeing on the meaning isn't the goal; instead, you win by generating as many answers and options as possible. Let this round of the game open doors and suggest direction; think of this as an opportunity to envision your perfect mutual future.

Winning the Game

Did you step outside your routine? Did you generate just one romantic idea you can implement this week? Did you come up with just one tiny gift idea? Did you renew your commitment to mutual growth? Did you actually manage to set aside a single hour of your week to spend a little time thinking exclusively about each other? Did you sweep the cards off the table, tackle your partner, and score a home run for the Love Team?

If any of the above happened—in fact, if your efforts earned you nothing more than a wink, a smooch, and a playful squeeze—you win!

Whenever routine reduces you to going through the motions, grab your partner, grab the nearest tarot deck, and deal yourself some alternatives to the daily grind. Play Tarot for Two, and you'll be surprised just how often you'll find romance in the cards.

A Closer Look At:
The Bright Idea Deck

Created by Mark McElroy
Illustrated by Eric Hotz

- 78 full-color cards and a 216-page illustrated book

- Cards are 2¾ x 4¾ with reversible backs and illustrated pips

- Uses bold, contemporary art to jumpstart the brainstorming process

- Card titles and descriptions are designed to generate ideas, expand creative expression, and stimulate thought processes

- Designed to work as both a divinatory tarot deck and a mainstream brainstorming tool

Living La Vida Arcana

Beyond the Celtic Cross

by Thalassa

I t eventually becomes apparent that the tarot lifestyle consists of many things beyond reading the cards for self and others. After a time it becomes clear that there is a great deal more to the tarot than amazing your friends and confounding your pets with brightly colored pieces of pasteboard. You reach the point when the books are read; you can do a mean Horseshoe Spread; you have discovered your life, destiny, and get-out-of-jail-free cards; and the intuitive edge appears to be sharpening nicely—which is about the time when you're run over by the "Now What?" Express. This is also exactly the time to have fun, hang loose, and let the endless ageless wisdom tickle your ear with its unheard voice. Those who take the Art & Science of Divination too seriously do themselves a disservice. If you listen carefully, you can the hear the chortle of the cosmos: life is seldom fair, but it's often funny. If the gods didn't have a sense of humor, they wouldn't have made platypi, penguins, or sex. If the universe didn't enjoy doing a Dance of the Seven Veils, the tarot would never have evolved.

Beyond its divinatory capacity, the tarot is a toolbox for plumbing the subconscious, an aid and guide to the meditation and mystery traditions of the West, a triggering device for associative thought, an oracular information system (a magical familiar! a dessert topping! a rainy day spiritual project! but we digress). Ideally, there comes a point when the images of the tarot cease to be pictures on laminated cardboard and become—for lack of a better term—part of the taro-tist's DNA. The symbols, associations, and personal meanings you incorporate seep in—like astral butter into the nooks and crannies of a metaphysical English muffin—to occupy all the levels of the person. Essentially, you become the tarot and the tarot becomes you.

The leap that takes the neophyte from the basic reading skill set to life-enriching obsession can be seen as a sort of off-road, all-ter-rain process. You take off across the less-traveled and even uncharted realms of the mind using the cards as a sort of meta-physical sports utility vehicle.

When you start to feel uncomfortable or stilted by the meanings you've pounded into your head, or feel ready to look a little deeper, try this exercise. Be prepared to see the images of the tarot every-where. Don't go consciously looking for them; just be prepared to see everything and anything through the lens of the tarot. Enjoy the unfolding of the images within and around you. To use an example from this writer's life, in the Swingin' '60s, soon after I started my own explorations on the Royal Road, a friend of mine wanted to start studying tarot too. We went to Ye Olde Local Metaphysical Supply House to buy her a deck of her own. Shiny new pack of *Albano-Waite* in hand, we adjourned to a nearby park to make intro-ductions. As we began to shuffle the crisp and slightly sticky arcana, a young man in colorful but tattered clothes (it was the '60s, after all) suddenly appeared and strolled past us, rucksack on his shoulder, small brown and white dog yapping happily at his heels. It was the first time—although certainly not the last—I saw a trump image manifest in the material world, and my first intimation that this stuff worked on more levels of meaning than I had previ-ously been aware of. This sort of phenomenon has happened time and again, sometimes subtly, just as often not. It needn't be spec-tacular to have meaning, but admittedly, the show often gets pretty darned interesting.

The tarot seems custom-made to stir the both preverbal and visual minds, both of which are stimulated by drama and emotion as much as by symbols and images. This ability to resonate on so many levels accounts for much of the tarot's exhaustless fascina-tion for artists, psychologists, directors of cheesy thrillers, divina-tion hotline operators, and devoted practitioners of all sorts. There is a fluidity to the images that provokes inspiration, regardless of

the execution of the artwork (a blessing in the case of several tarot decks currently in the marketplace). The associative skills used in reading and studying the tarot foster echoes in other corridors of the mind, and it is not an exaggeration to say that the tarot can alter consciousness.

There is no end to what you can do with the tarot in a spirit that combines play and serious exploration (which this author considers one of the best ways to deeply learn something). Try using the cards to ask the questions as well as provide the answers. Tell stories using the cards as characters and situations; current research indicates that this was one of the earliest uses of the cards way back in the Renaissance. Play "free association theater" with the cards: permit the conscious and unconscious to yield personal layers and interpretations of the images and symbols. This is especially good when acclimating yourself to a new deck, or rekindling bonds with a deck that you haven't used recently.

On a more whimsical note (but still efficacious—trust your writer on this), try reading with cocktail napkins, index cards, poker chips, postcards, even a deck you dislike or don't resonate with (this author has discovered some remarkable insights while being forced by circumstances into using decks at which she ordinarily turns up her nose—that wacky side of the universe manifesting itself yet again). Let the blank (or repugnant) surfaces trigger deeper levels of awareness.

Play with your cards early and often. Look at them in different lights. Take them apart and put them back where you didn't find them. Use them as cosmic coffee filters for the constant stream of energy flowing from the Oracular Universe. Leave them in library books, hotel bibles, and bus stops to spread the mystery and mayhem to others, like a pebble dropped in a deceptively limpid pool. Use your past to understand your present. Ride bareback with the Knight of Swords. Chuck the King of Cups under the chin. Take tea with the Emperor and make him curl his pinky. Play strip poker with the Hermit. Book yourself a Knight at the Hyatt Tower. Take the keys to the Chariot and turn it in at the Stars. Sit in with Gabriel for a jam at the Judgement Jazz Café. You get the idea. If you are prepared to open yourself to it, this stuff works in remarkable ways, often without you needing to consciously try.

Heck, this stuff works. Period.

The Magician

Practical Applications

IL MAGO
LE BATELEUR

I

THE MAGICIAN
EL MAGO

DER MAGIER

DE MAGIËR

Going Pro

by James Wells

There comes a point in many people's tarot journeys when they decide to read the cards for a living, whether full-time or part-time. It's not for everybody. Many of my friends and students elect to use the cards only for themselves and their intimate circle of loved ones. However, if you've chosen to take the Fool's leap into the abyss of professional tarot consulting, this article is for you. As this is a vast topic, any tips and exercises herein are merely springboards, albeit important ones, based on personal experience. I'll focus on the qualities of a good professional tarot consultant, five key questions to answer before starting out, promotion, setting fees, and location.

Helpful Qualities

What qualities are woven into the fabric of a good tarot professional? Competence, curiosity, ethics, humility, and self-awareness.

Competence

A tarot professional knows his or her tool and craft well before offering any services to the public. It sounds elementary, but I've seen some very shabby readers charge money for a skill they have not yet grasped. Read the best tarot books, join an Internet group, attend workshops and conferences, take classes, practice on yourself and others, know your cards inside out. There's no rush—I began to explore tarot in 1979 and didn't charge a professional fee until 1994.

Also, part of being competent is not scattering your attention. A client's confidence in your tarot abilities will not be kindled if they see that you also "specialize" in runes, palmistry, tea leaves, scrying, astrology, archangelic healing, and hepatoscopy. Focus! Do one to three things well rather than ten things poorly. It's also helpful to relate your tarot knowledge to, or derive more tarot knowledge from, other disciplines—psychology, mythology, literature, and so forth.

Curiosity

Curiosity is important. A good tarot reader aches to know the questions behind the questions. If you're curious enough to probe deeper, it will rub off on your clients. They'll ask richer questions, which will lead to more constructive answers and a more enjoyable interaction for both parties. Your curiosity should also prompt you to explore what's new in tarot. Investigate the latest books, newest decks, most recent historical theories, and twenty-first–century applications.

Ethics

The Compleat Tarot Professional is ethical. Be conscious of what you do and don't do as a tarot reader, and be comfortable saying so out loud. As an ethical reader, you quote your fees and stick with them. You're clear about session durations before the appointment begins. The ethical tarot consultant does *not* predict death or dire illness. Period! Nor does she or he offer unsolicited intuitive information. Several times, people have walked up to me (usually in metaphysical bookstores) to tell me there's a spiritual message that they absolutely *have to* convey to me. My response has generally been, "No, you don't." It's bad manners and a bad ego trip. Don't do it. Period!

An ethical tarot reader only does what she or he is qualified to do. If you're not a trained lawyer, psychologist, homeopath, accountant, physician, or other nondivinatory professional, don't dispense advice that is better left to those who know what they're doing. Keep a list of names and the contact information of non-tarot practitioners so that you can refer querents to these other resources as needed.

Ethical tarot consultants do not make judgment calls on a client's choices, behaviors, lifestyle, financial status, sexual orientation, gender, and so forth. It is not your job to convert people to your spiritual or moral worldview, but rather to simply provide helpful information. Neither is manipulation a good thing. To use a reading to push your own agenda will have the Karma Police on your butt so fast, it won't be funny.

An ethical tarot reader knows his or her boundaries around third-party readings. Will you or won't you read for an absent person that a client inquires about?

And lastly, ethics demand that you don't blab about people's sessions behind their backs, no matter how juicy the information may be. Confidentiality is always courteous.

Humility

The ideal professional reader is humble. Anyone who declares that he is 100 percent accurate (whatever "accurate" means) is either lying or deluded. We're human, we make mistakes, and we're not perfect. Get a hard helmet and deal with it. Humility also incorporates the realization that a tarot session is not an epic dog-and-pony show with you as its reigning star. A reading is a co-created experience made up of you, the client, the cards, the topic, the questions or spread positions, and the presence of whatever you believe your source of wisdom to be.

Self-awareness

A self-aware tarot practitioner is a good tarot practitioner. Work on yourself. Healers and counselors need healing and counseling too. If you plan to be of any use to those who seek guidance in your consulting room, you need to be as clear and healthy for them, and for yourself, as possible. Go to analysis, see a therapist from time to time, talk with another professional, explore your dreams, do honest journal work, go for massage and energy work. Your clients will thank you for it.

Five Key Questions

Before opening your professional tarot practice, go through the list of questions provided below and respond to them in writing. Answer them in the order presented. Be honest. Ask and answer these five questions once a year to check in with yourself and your business.

For extra clarification and inspiration, turn these questions into a tarot spread and pull cards for them. Do this only after you've answered them on your own.

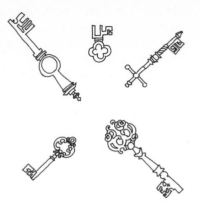

1) Who are you as a person? List your strengths and weaknesses, personality traits, people skills, philosophy of life, likes and dislikes, etc.

2) As a tarot reader, what do you do? What special trait, technique, or tool sets you apart from the rest? What's your consultation style? Some readers are interactive while others do all of the talking. Some are predictive while others are therapeutic. One may be peppy and another colleague may be very quiet. Some consultants enhance their tarot practice with other modalities in which they're trained, such as flower essences, herbs, essential oils, movement, dance, energy healing, or guided imagery. One might work methodically, card-by-card, while another might simply toss a bunch of cards on the table to trigger psychic insights.

3) What is your mission statement as a tarot professional? Be clear, in one sentence, about why you do this. For example: to facilitate the process of choice through a blend of intuition and intellect; to assist people to see symbolic patterns and how they play out in their lives; to yank people's thinking out of the box in creative yet practical ways.

4) What benefits do/can people derive from a session with you? What's in it for *them*? Make a list of these benefits. For example: people experience a focused sense of direction; they realize how wise they truly are; clients are forewarned, therefore forearmed; they feel relaxed and lighter; people see their options more clearly, so they can choose more efficiently.

5) Who would benefit from your tarot services? Brainstorm a list of people who would resonate with your personality, your reading style, your mission statement, and your benefits. Take into consideration age, gender, profession, income bracket, hobbies, location, and so forth. A few hours later, go back to your list and narrow it down to three or four. These people are your target market.

Promoting Your Business

Your answers in the previous section are the building blocks for promoting yourself. You now have a target market: a specific set of people you want to reach out to. This will save you a great deal of time, energy, and money, because you won't scatter your marketing efforts willy-nilly. You'll be focused. Your business cards, brochures, classified ads, flyers, and display ads will contain words, phrases, and imagery which not only reflect the essence of your services, but will also appeal to the three or four groups you've chosen.

In all of your printed literature, be sure to highlight the benefits, not yourself. The general public is not interested in your life story, scintillating though it may be. Neither do they care that you're a ninety-third generation psychic trained by ascended Pleadean tarot masters at the Egyptian Academy of Timeless Truth. Keep the bio to a maximum of three or four sentences. People want to know what's in it for them!

The general public is also lazy. Don't bombard them with too much text. Keep your written material brief and to the point. Fonts should be clean and easy to read, so no frilly pseudo-Gothic scripts in varying shades of pink. Leave enough blank space to keep it tidy.

Find out where your target people shop, live, eat, and socialize. Leave your printed materials in or near these places. Also find out which publications they read. Place your ads in them. Know their favorite radio and television stations. Get yourself an interview on them. What organizations do these people belong to? Send a letter of introduction suggesting that you give a talk at one of their meetings. What causes are close to your potential clients' hearts? Donate gift certificates to their favorite charity auction. Speak at their local library. Be omnipresent!

Setting Fees

This is simultaneously everybody's most and least favorite topic. Some people say that one should not charge a fee for what they believe is a "spiritual" service. Fie on them! The day that landlords don't charge rent, supermarkets give away food, and university education is gratis is the day I won't charge for a tarot consultation.

Part of knowing what to charge is based on your target market's income bracket, but it's also based on whether you're in an urban, suburban, or rural area. It also depends on how much money per year you'd like to earn from your tarot work and how many clients you're willing to work with every week. Remember too that the only things that people are paying for are your time and expertise, not the content of the reading. A person recently asked me, "What do I get for $150?" to which I responded, "An hour of my time."

A rough formula for setting your fee is:

desired yearly income divided by 52 = x
x divided by number of desired number of clients per week = y
round off y to the nearest number ending with five or zero

Here are a couple of examples. Madeleine decides that her target market includes bank CEOs and architects. She figures that $100 to $200 per hour is an appropriate fee range. Madeleine would like to earn $50,000 per year from tarot consultations and work with up to eight clients per week.

$50,000 divided by 52 = 961.53
$961.53 divided by 8 = 120.19

Madeleine decides to charge $120 for an hour-long consultation.

Herman wants to work with college students and stay-at-home parents. He feels that $60 to $100 per hour is a fair range for his desired clientele. He's willing to work with a maximum of 10 people per week and would like to earn $40,000 per year.

$40,000 divided by 52 = 769.23
$769.23 divided by 10 = 76.923

Herman chooses to charge $75 for his hour-long sessions.

If you'd rather not do all of that math, then a fair price to begin with is one dollar per minute.

Where?

You now have your well-honed tarot skills, promotional material, a set fee, and a clientele. Where do you intend to offer your consultations? I work in my home, seeing clients and students in the living room where I also do sessions over the phone for out-of-province or international querents. Three or four times a month, I offer "meet-the-public" readings at a large metaphysical bookstore. It suits my personality to work from home, with the occasional excursion elsewhere. Many other options exist, though.

The plusses of working at home are that there's no extra overhead to pay, you're in your own familiar space, it's easy to make people feel at home, it's private and safe (assuring confidentiality), and you don't have to schlep across town. Potential pitfalls might be inviting total strangers into your home, not getting out of the house enough, household distractions such as laundry (ha! Not in my house), housemates or significant others who inhibit a sense of privacy, and having to keep the place somewhat presentable.

Some readers like to do housecalls. It keeps their home address unknown, it gets them out of the house, and they get a better feel for the people in their own surroundings. The down side of housecalls is having to get there, especially if you're in a northern clime, in midwinter. There are also safety issues around visiting a new person's home. If you decide to do housecalls, leave the name, number, and address of the person you're visiting with someone you know.

A metaphysical bookstore has the advantage of being a neutral space. You're more likely to find a sympathetic audience here and meet new people to add to your client base. This option also gets you out of the house. Problems include not being able to charge as much (proprietors want people to buy products, not blow all their money on a reading), being subject to the store's policies and rules, less privacy (even with a curtain or booth), and the fact that metaphysical bookstores occasionally attract wackos who want to explain to you how they're the product of a half-human half-Venusian marriage.

Another possible workspace is a coffeehouse or tea room. One of my colleagues does quite well by doing readings in upscale hotels during afternoon tea. It's an enjoyable and elegant way to work. Draw-backs are the lack of privacy and the need to charge a lower fee. One generally can't go as in-depth during these consultations either. No maitre d'hôtel wants to see his paying guests break down at some profound, soul-shaking discovery.

You could also rent office space shared by another professional—masseur, psychotherapist, astrologer, etc.—on certain days of the week when it's not in use by them. This has the plusses of lower rent, potential for cross-referrals, and having your professional days scheduled in advance. You might also get a receptionist to take appointments for you. The shared office could be a problem if you're there alone, if the other people don't want you to display your brochures or business cards on your days off, if there's a fundamentalist receptionist who wants to burn you and your cards, and if there's very little chance to expand your office hours.

Three final options do not rank among my favorites, but I offer them here anyhow. These are psychic fairs, parties, and psychic phone lines. While there are some very good practitioners involved, these options generally attract a clientele who have a "show me" attitude and who are searching for spooky entertainment or quick fixes rather than tools and processes that can assist them to take more responsibility for their own lives.

Professional tarot reading is a terrific opportunity to share your passion for tarot and your hard-won reading skills with a vast array of interesting and wonderful people. It won't be all almonds and roses, but then what is? It's possible to earn a good living through offering your tarot services, but be prepared to be patient and to work at it. It's not an overnight success story. But the myriad rewards, both internal and tangible, are truly worth it. I wish you well!

Ask a Better Question

by Mark McElroy

I get all sorts of queries when I read for clients, and during a recent series of free public readings, people raised the following questions:

- "When will my settlement check finally arrive?"
- "Why doesn't Terri love me back?"
- "Is my daughter about to get a divorce?"
- "Is Kevin secretly gay?"

They also asked questions like these:

- "How can I start saving more and spending less?"
- "How can I find a more fulfilling relationship?"
- "What can I do to help my daughter through her divorce?"
- "What can I do to let Kevin know he can trust me to be his friend, regardless?"

The first list of questions captures my clients' initial attempts to voice their questions. The second list records how the same clients phrased the same questions five minutes later. What made the difference? In those five minutes, we shared some simple techniques designed to emphasize action, take responsibility for creating

change, and open our minds to unexpected solutions.

Why invest time and energy in revising these inquiries? Did teaching freshman-level English leave me unable to resist the urge to critique my clients' questions? Do I fancy myself a puppet master, reducing my clients to ventriloquist dummies by forcing them to ask only what I want them to ask?

Not at all. I help my clients frame their questions more effectively for one reason: I want them to leave our session feeling empowered and ready for action.

Divination, after all, is an effort to tap into the divine. (Someone I know once described the process as "like prayer, but with faster feedback.") Shouldn't getting in touch with the divine better align us with a larger plan . . . and give us a plan of action, as well? After consulting the cards, shouldn't we feel more confident, better prepared, more capable, and more certain that we're headed in the best possible direction?

I think so . . . and, over the years, I've discovered that clients feel more empowered when we put at least as much energy into phrasing their questions as we do into interpreting the cards. The principle is simple: ask better questions, get better answers.

Reprehensible . . . or Responsible?

Some readers take real exception to the idea of helping clients revise their questions.

I know a young woman—an experienced reader, with many clients all over the globe—who insists that tarot readers should *never* encourage the revision of questions. "I never, ever rephrase a question," she says. "The client is asking what he or she feels led to ask, and it's my responsibility to get that person an answer, period. People who encourage clients to rephrase questions aren't client-focused. They're insisting someone say a certain thing in a certain way before allowing them access to the cards. Who am I to say that some questions are better than others?"

That's certainly one approach! After years of reading for the public, though, I'm on the opposite end of the spectrum.

For many of my clients, sitting for a reading represents their first effort to deal with a challenge, concern, or situation. Often, they've been plagued by a problem for a very long time. Caught up in that energy, they struggle to put their feelings into words. As a result, their first efforts are often more shaped by frustration than by focus. Here's an example of how Jenna, a college sophomore, first phrased her question:

"I'm just tired of dealing with my boyfriend's temper. He makes such a big deal out of every little thing. I can't do anything right. It wasn't always like this, and—don't get me wrong—sometimes things are still really good. But I catch myself walking on eggshells all the time I'm around him, because I don't want to say the wrong thing and spoil the moment. I guess my question is: will things ever go back to how they were?"

Can you feel Jenna's frustration here? Her heartbreak? Her fear? Jenna's first attempt to deal with these strong emotions produces a straightforward Yes/No question. Would generating an answer to this question be the best thing to do for Jenna?

Let's say the cards indicate that, yes, things will eventually go back to how they were. What is Jenna supposed to do in the meantime—suffer through more abuse while waiting for a brighter future? And what if the relationship does improve, but takes decades to do so? What is Jenna supposed to do then? Comfort herself with the mantra, "This, too, shall pass"?

Conversely, what if the cards say "No, this situation won't ever improve." (I'm inclined to agree, but that's beside the point!) What should Jenna do then? Stop trying? Break things off? Decide that, if she wants to remain with this boyfriend, she's just going to have to commit to a life of constant trepidation?

In addition to her frustration, Jenna's question was also affected by misinformation about how tarot works. She had no idea, for example, that tarot could be used for anything more than "Yes or No" questions. She also believed, as many other clients (and, to be fair, some readers) do, that tarot could be used to pinpoint the exact second of the exact day when a specific event would occur—the arrival of a check in the mail, for example.

Working exclusively with Jenna's first Yes/No question commits us to generating an answer with no more detail, depth, or clarity than we'd get from Magic 8-Ball . . . or from the toss of a coin. Given tarot's rich vocabulary of images and scope of nuance, I think that's a tragedy in itself.

Ultimately, as a reader, you must decide what your approach will be. Will you answer whatever question is put to you, exactly as your client suggested it? Or will you, to some degree, help your clients explore the more effective questions lurking behind their first attempt to frame their feelings with words?

Personally and professionally, I feel an obligation—more of a calling, really—to put whatever degree of knowledge, intuition, and insight I've been blessed with to work for my clients. For me, that includes helping them phrase the best possible questions.

So What Makes One Question Better than the Other?

Good question!

No, really: the question above really is a good question. Unlike so many questions, it's specific. Asking a question like, "What makes one question better than another?" prompts us to expect a list of standards we can use to distinguish the pros and cons associated with a certain type of question.

My approach to tarot emphasizes personal empowerment, so I encourage my clients to explore opportunities to pursue their own best possible futures. For us, then, the "better" questions avoid fatalistic, coin-flipping, Yes/No outlooks on life.

With that criteria in mind, spotting empowering questions is easy, because they always:

1) **Lead to action.** In most cases, this means favoring questions that start with *What* and *How* instead of questions that start with *Why* and *When*.

Let's say we're working with a client who initially wants to know why she's constantly at odds with her mother. Perhaps, after pulling a few cards, we discover that, in a previous life, the two women were bitter business rivals. (Hey, it could happen!) That makes a great story . . . but knowing the origin of her emotions won't eliminate them—or provide her with a strategy for dealing more effectively with her mother today.

Or perhaps a client wants to know when he'll get a long-awaited promotion at work, and the spread indicates the promotion is four months away. Will slacking off now (after all, he's getting a promotion in four months, anyway) affect that outcome? Would working harder accelerate the process at all? Must my client resign himself to being swept along like a leaf in a river, with no ability to influence the course of events at all?

By contrast, *What* and *How* questions empower clients by emphasizing strategy and action. "What can I do to deal more effectively with my mother?" produces a series of steps a client can take with an eye toward improving that relationship. "How can I speed my advancement up the corporate ladder?" encourages a client to take an active role in shaping his own future.

To encourage clients to ask active questions, I often post a sign at my reading table: "Step One: Begin your question with the words 'What can I do about . . .' or 'How can I . . .'" As a result, my clients often adopt the language of empowerment . . . even before they sit down with me!

2) Incorporate personal responsibility. This is easy to do: just make sure your clients use the word "I" in their questions!

Some of my clients think the tarot is the metaphysical equivalent of those tiny, wireless spy cams advertised on the Internet. Is Clara cheating on me? How does Mannie really feel about me? What is Rico really doing this weekend?

"Hey," I like to say, "I'm a tarot reader, not a private detective!" Rather than turn our session into an episode of *The Jerry Springer Show*, I encourage these clients to approach the same issues from the perspective of personal responsibility: How can I put my concerns about an unfaithful partner to rest? What can I do to encourage Mannie to tell me how he really feels? How can I deal more effectively with my anxiety about Rico's secrecy?

Others clients, perhaps in an effort to avoid feelings of guilt, project responsibility for their challenges onto other people. Why does Robert constantly sabotage our relationship? Why does my wife always pick fights right before a family vacation? What's wrong with Barry, anyway?

I remind these clients that the only attitudes and actions we can control are our own: "Rather than focus on this other person, let's explore the situation from the perspective of what *you* can control." What does the constant tension in my relationship with Robert indicate? How can I contribute to healthier, happier, less dramatic family vacations? How can I let Barry know I'm here for him?

When clients bring me questions focused on others, I say, "Asking a question with the word 'I' in it empowers you by giving you more control over the situation. How can you rephrase your question so that it includes the word 'I'?"

3) Explore options. Clients frequently become so focused on one goal that they ignore all other options and outcomes. As a result, they load their questions with assumptions that blind them to other possibilities:

- When will Jeff ask me to marry him? (Maybe he won't.)

- How can I get that job at Speedy Print? (Pursuing that one job might prevent you from finding one that would pay more and be better aligned with your personal goals.)

- What should I buy for Sharon's birthday? (Maybe Sharon would appreciate a handmade gift even more!)

As a reader, I listen for these assumptions and suggest alternatives. To do this, I engage my clients in a discussion about goals. To what extent could you be happy with Jeff outside of marriage? How does working at Speedy Print move you closer to your professional goals? What's more important to you: making a quick purchase, or delighting Sharon?

Want another way to help clients explore options? Try "Option Cards." When constructing a spread, add three option cards representing alternative outcomes your client is inclined to overlook. Working with option cards suggests new directions, clarifies goals, and prompts insights, simply by asking the question, "What if you tried this instead?"

4) Seek guidance, not control. Setting and pursuing goals is critical to my empowerment-centered approach, but choosing the wrong goals (selfish goals, for example, or goals that ultimately work against our growth and health) and pursing them willy-nilly would be anything but empowering.

When clients ask questions that amount to "How can I get what I want?", it's often profitable to ask how this immediate goal fits in with plans for their long-term happiness. You can do this in a number of gentle ways:

- If you and your client are comfortable doing so, begin the session with a prayer or invocation that positions the reading as a humble, receptive approach to exploring the best and brightest future.

- Especially if you believe divination is an effort to align ourselves with the divine, ask the client to talk about the goal in terms of his or her higher power's plan for his or her life. (You might also draw a card designed to represent the higher power's commentary on the client's plan.)

- Ask whether the client is open to drawing "Advice Cards"—suggestions from the universe designed to answer questions such as "What's the healthiest possible course of action?" or "What would the most selfless choice be?"—in addition to the cards in the primary spread.

A reading encourages a more thoughtful approach to life . . . and also offers an opportunity to examine our options from a more noble perspective. If you share my belief that the ultimate empowerment comes from aligning ourselves with our own best path, then you might want to share strategies like these with your clients.

The Ultimate Question: What's Next?

Ultimately, only you can decide the extent to which you want to help clients frame their questions. If you decide you feel called to "take 'em as they come," by all means do so!

I don't think anyone can deny, though, that as readers we have a special and deeply personal relationship with our oracles of choice. My experience gives me insight not only into the tarot, but also into the questions I feel provide the best possible results.

When I read the cards for others, I feel called to bring all my talents to bear on the issues my clients share. By encouraging clients to ask questions that encourage action, emphasize personal responsibility, explore options, and seek guidance, I become a more active partner in my clients' quests for healthier, more rewarding lives.

For me, that means giving them access to my intuition, my knowledge of the cards and their potential meanings . . . and my faith (informed by years of experience as a corporate problem-solver and project planner) in the transformative power of empowering questions.

Psychic Fairs, Public Readings

by Corrine Kenner

I f you have ever been to a psychic fair, you've probably seen any number of tarot readers, lined up in rows, giving readings from tidy little tables. You might even have thought about offering tarot readings yourself at a festival or a fundraiser for your favorite nonprofit group.

It's a lot of fun to read tarot cards in public. The atmosphere is charged with excitement. Clients are enthusiastic. What's more, your skills as a reader are tested, stretched, and ultimately strengthened. You can discover techniques in public that you would never develop in the comfort of your living room.

At the same time, however, public readings can be demanding. Customers expect you to be clear, concise, accurate—and fast. You might give more readings in a day than you would ordinarily handle in a month. And you will probably have to work in a noisy, frenetic space, in full view of onlookers and passersby.

If you would like to try your hand at reading tarot in public, here are some tips I picked up by doing readings in public places, and by watching how other tarot readers work.

1. Be prepared. Gather everything you will need the day before you plan to do public readings.

2. Be yourself. You don't need to wear a costume (unless you want to), or talk in an accent, or pretend to be someone you're not. Just read the cards for others as you would read them for a friend.

3. Use a tarot deck you really like, and make sure you're comfortable with all of the symbols and images on the cards.

4. Dress comfortably. You might be doing some heavy setup work before the fair begins, and then find yourself sitting for hours on end once your readings start.

5. Decide beforehand how you would like to manage your time. You could offer to answer one or two specific questions for a single preset price. Many readers simply offer five, ten, or fifteen-minute readings, which are easy to price—and they help keep long-winded clients from monopolizing your time.

6. Feel free to ask other tarot readers what they charge, and price your readings accordingly. $1 a minute seems to be a common rate. (At the same time, decide whether you will accept checks or work on a cash-only basis.)

7. Post a sign that advertises your services and prices. Be specific, so people passing by can see at a glance what you offer, how much it costs, and what they will get out of the deal. One weekend, at a festival in St. Paul, I used a sign that read, "Tarot Readings: $20 / Your career / Your love life / Your friends and family." I printed it out from my computer, framed it in a plastic holder from an office supply store, and set it on my tarot table.

8. Try to recruit an assistant to help manage your waiting customers. Otherwise, post a sign-up sheet for people who want readings.

9. If you are just one of a large number of psychic readers, and you don't have a steady stream of clients, you might feel self-conscious. Just offer free one-card readings if business slows down. You'll get more customers—and you'll have more fun.

10. Be friendly. Don't pressure anyone, but don't be afraid to ask passersby if they'd like a tarot reading. Some people just need to be invited to the table.

11. Also, be prepared to deal with a smart aleck or two. Smile and offer to read them their cards; that will scare most of the crackpots away.

12. Use your time in public to promote your private readings. Bring business cards and brochures, and hand them out between readings. Also, be sure to hand a business card to everyone who gets a reading from you.

13. If you are a professional reader or teacher, invite your customers to sign up for your mailing list. Also, include a space for names, addresses, e-mail, and phone numbers on your sign-up list.

14. Try to arrange your space so that you create a buffer of privacy for each client.

15. Personally, I like to keep public readings light and uplifting. Time is limited, after all, and I don't think it's appropriate to do deep, dark, hardcore tarot in public places. If you find yourself with someone who needs a more serious session, offer to follow up with a private reading later.

16. If you find that you are especially sensitive to other people's moods, do some shielding and grounding meditations before you begin your readings.

17. Between readings, breathe deeply to clear your mind and shuffle the cards to clear your deck.

18. Drink water or hot tea while you read, to keep your voice smooth and supple.

19. Bring breath mints. If your throat gets dry or you feel a little nervous, you'll probably need them.

20. Stop for lunch or a snack when you read for extended periods.

21. Take a break every two hours. Get up, stretch your back, neck, and shoulders, and walk around for five minutes. If you stay hunched over your table for hours on end, you are bound to feel stiff and sore the next day.

22. Set a time to go home. Don't feel compelled to stay until you've worked for everyone who wants a reading. Bring along your appointment book, and offer to schedule private readings for a later date.

The Traveling Tarot Reader's Supply List

Before you head off to a psychic fair or festival, make sure you plan ahead and pack your gypsy wagon with all of the tools you might need. If you will be carrying all of your supplies yourself, remember to choose lightweight items.

Basic Supplies

There is some basic equipment you can't do without—tarot cards, for example. Try to bring two or three decks, so you can offer clients a choice or switch as the spirit moves you. Choose decks that depict people from a range of ethnic backgrounds, so that every client can identify with the images. And remember that you'll be working in public, where sweet-faced children and little old ladies can see your cards. Make sure your decks are "G" or "PG"-rated.

- At most psychic fairs, a table is included with your space rental. If not, try using a three-legged accent table from a discount store—the round kind, with the screw-in legs. They're sturdy, they're portable, and they're cheap. Small card tables also work well.

- Like tables, chairs are often included with your booth space. If you need to bring your own, bring a couple of lightweight camping chairs or plastic stacking chairs.

- If you plan to set time limits on readings, you will need a clock, a watch, or a timer.

- Bring a sign-in sheet, pens, and a clipboard, for crowd control.

- If you are set up to take credit cards, bring along your credit card machine and blank receipts.

- Don't forget a moneybag or cash box for your earnings. It's a good idea to bring something that's small enough to slip into your purse or bag if you decide to take a break away from your table.

- Put some starting change in your moneybag, too. You should probably price your readings in $5 or $10 increments, because most people will have $5 and $10 bills on hand. Make sure you have enough initial cash on hand, however, to make change for the first few clients who pay with $20 bills.

- If you are a professional, you may need a receipt book to stay on the up-and-up with the tax collector.

- And if your prices vary or if you're charging state or local tax, you may need a calculator.

Decorations

Your area will seem more appealing with a few decorative items:

- Bring tablecloths, spread cloths, scarves, and fabric to drape over tables, chairs, and dividers. Fabric is one of the easiest, most effective ways to decorate your reading area —and it's easy to carry, too.

- If open flame is allowed, bring candles and matches.

- You might want to use a small table lamp to brighten your reading area.

- Some tarot readers decorate their space with crystals, flowers, and decorative figurines.

- If you want background music, bring a portable stereo and CDs or tapes.

- You can soften your seating area with chair cushions or throws.

- You might want to entice passersby with candy in attractive candy dishes.

- And don't forget to bring tissue, for the weepers.

Pro Style

A few finishing touches will make you look like a pro:

- Bring business cards and a holder to display them. You can print out your own business cards on pre-designed stock, or order inexpensive cards from online printing services.

- If you have advertising brochures, put them where people

can pick them up—even if you're busy giving readings. Make it easy for new clients to call you for readings or classes.

- Your booth rental might include a banner or a sign, but it will probably be a boring black-and-white printout. Design a colorful poster to attract business—the larger, the better.

- If you position your sign on an easel near the front of your booth, prospective customers can see at a glance what you have to offer.

- Also, post a complete list of your services and prices somewhere near your table.

- If you are working without a crowd-control assistant, bring a small table to hold your sign-up list.

- Bring a "Back in 10 minutes" sign to leave out while you're on break.

- Make a name for yourself. You might get a badge or nametag from the organizers, but just in case, bring your own. That way, everyone can see that you're working.

- If you plan to provide tapes of each reading, bring a tape recorder with a clip-on microphone. Don't forget blank cassette tapes, extra batteries, and a power supply.

- If you want to raffle off a free reading or gift as an incentive, bring a raffle bowl and raffle slips for people to fill out with their names, addresses, and phone numbers. You can add their contact information to your mailing list later.

Tools

Don't forget the tools you will need to set up and maintain your space. You can—and should—practice setting up your booth at home, just to get an idea of the basic supplies you'll want on hand. Festivals are filled with surprises, however. Just to be safe, bring all of the tools on this list; you probably won't know exactly what you'll need until you get there.

- Extension cords
- Scissors
- Scotch tape
- Masking tape
- Duct tape
- Tacks, nails, and a hammer
- Pliers
- Safety pins
- Staples and a stapler
- Wire
- Removable hooks or clips for securing signs and drapery
- Blank paper or poster board, in case you need to make a last-minute sign
- A permanent marker
- Spray cleaner
- Paper towels
- Wet wipes

Spreads for Public Readings

While you can adapt your favorite spreads for public readings, you should probably forget about the full-length Celtic Cross: public readings are rushed, and long, complicated spreads will probably be out of the question. Aim for quality, not quantity, in your readings. Plan to read three or four cards per person—and remember that you can always expand on them, if necessary.

Here are three basic spreads you can use to start:

- Past-Present-Future. Shuffle, and ask your client to cut the deck into three piles. Discuss the top card in each stack, relating it to the past, present, and future of the question. Then flip over each stack and discuss the bottom card as a secret or unconscious factor.

- Condensed Celtic Cross. Shuffle and deal just the first seven cards of the classic Celtic Cross: the significator (your client), the covering card (your client's situation), the crossing card (new influences), the foundation (your client's perspective), the recent past, the near future, and the crowning card (the most likely outcome).

- The Spread of the Elements. Shuffle and ask your client to cut the deck into four piles. Each one can represent strengths or suggestions for improvement in a single area of life: spiritual, emotional, intellectual, and physical. Each stack also corresponds to a suit of the Minor Arcana: wands, cups, swords, and pentacles.

Reading tarot cards in public truly is a lot of fun—especially when you plan ahead, and come prepared to enjoy your time in the spotlight.

Those Scary Cards

by Winter Wren

When you set up shop as a tarot reader, you open the door to many types of seekers at your reading table. Some are aware of the deeper nature of the tarot and seek to learn more about the journey within themselves. Others come to gain better understanding of the choices along their life paths. Still others seek out merely the stereotypical fortune-teller; someone who will tell them what is coming and when. They come for the entertainment value more than for growth or awareness.

These seekers often come into the reading expecting dim lighting, many candles, too much incense, and a kaleidoscope of colors. Even serious seekers from more traditional religious backgrounds approach a reading with trepidation. This type of seeker sits on the edge of the chair across the table handling the cards nervously. "I don't want to see the Death card. That card is scary. It's not in here, right?" The friend who accompanies the seeker (so she need not face the news alone) shakes her head, "What about that Devil? He scares me." And so begins another session with seekers who want to know, yet do not want to know. They want their readers to tell them "only the good stuff"; to keep the scary Death, Devil, or Tower cards from showing up in the spread; to be told only what they want to hear: the nice aspects. In effect, they want to hear that their lives are going to go fine, with no responsibility or result from their own actions.

This is the perfect time for us, as tarot readers, to begin the awakening of our seekers—to steer them away from the "fortune-telling" aspects of tarot reading and direct them toward gaining ground in their lives. It opens a window of opportunity to introduce seekers to new concepts and ideas that provide them a glimpse of the world from a different viewpoint. A good tarot reader is a bridge to enlightenment for those who come seeking answers. Tarot is a tool of empowerment for gaining better control over one's own life. In order for the seekers to cross the bridge, the roadblocks have to come down. One of the greatest blocks is fear. Fear impedes learning and growth. Until a seeker addresses that fear, forward movement is blocked.

When working with seekers for the first time, it is my practice to talk with them for a bit before beginning the session. I do not wish to learn more about their lives or issues at this time; rather, I wish to learn about their perceptions of the tarot. By having a clearer understanding of the concerns a seeker brings to the table, I can better address those issues and begin to take down some barriers. Often those perceptions include strong, negative reactions to Death, the Devil, and the Tower. Now aware of the emotions invoked by those cards, I begin enlightening my seeker.

As tarot is my tool of choice in working with both students and seekers, I own a large variety of decks and keep them close at hand in my reading area. When a seeker expresses concern with these particular cards, I immediately pull several random decks from my collection. While I am sorting cards, I draw the seeker into a discussion of why he or she has such a strong impression of these cards—usually starting with the Death card, as it tends to evoke the strongest reaction.

Seekers express fears that the appearance of the Death card indicates that they are going to die soon or that someone they love will die. They view it as frightening and final. When it comes to the Devil, their feelings are more complex. Many view it from a stringent religious point of view that evokes concerns about the presence of evil in their lives. It is viewed as an indication that bad things are going to happen and that they cannot do anything about those bad things. The Tower card also brings up a level of fear: a fear of things being broken and destroyed, a fear of loss of what they hold dear.

As this discussion progresses, I pull those three cards from each of the decks, then lay them out in rows on the table. Faced with several artists' interpretations of the cards, the conversation will often stall. The things they fear lie on the table in front of them. They cannot deny the existence of the fear in their minds; they are staring at the root of that fear. Now the door is open, and we begin to change the negatives into positives. I compare and contrast images of the card from the various decks and, in the course of this comparison, inject mythology, lore, belief structures, and ideology surrounding the subject matter into the conversation.

Once again, I start with the Death card. Humans tend to view Death as the enemy, the one that cannot be defeated. I share with them other cultural ideas surrounding death, leading them to view death as both ending and beginning. Yes, the skeleton in the *Quest Tarot* appears rather aggressive and eager for victims. However, the portrayal of the Wild Hunt in the *Legends* deck is much less threatening to most and it gives me the opportunity to share with them the story of the Wild Hunt, which in turn allows me to start introducing seekers to the actual meanings of the Death card. I speak of transformation, of releasing what needs to pass from their lives in order for them to grow and move forward. From here, I progress to a more intermediate image of Death—perhaps the Banshee Crone from the *Faery Wicca* deck. We talk about the many cycles of life and how letting go of one aspect opens the doors to many new ones. I discuss with them the ideology behind the "unlucky thirteen" that accompanies the Death card, working to remove subconscious fears that prevent growth.

Death is a real event in each of our lives, something that tangibly exists, whereas the Devil presents a new set of challenges. The concerns around the Devil stem from the subconscious and are primarily rooted in Christian ideology—that of the fallen angel, a demon whose clutches humans must avoid. Things that go bump in the night are associated with evil. Some people incorporate them into scare tactics to keep children in line. Entertainment companies incorporate them to give us thrills.

13– The Banshee Crone

The Banshee Crone from the Faery Wicca Tarot

15 THE HORNED ONE

CERNUNNOS

The Horned One from Legend: The Arthurian Tarot

While the Devil himself may not be a tangible being, people see him as real because evil is real. They do not see the philosophy of the Devil in the guise of Pan, a creature of mischief. They do not embrace the chaotic atmosphere of the image.

The *Quest Tarot* Devil feeds well into that mythology. The card features things our culture equates to evil and dark forces: pitchforks, black cats, black roses, a reversed pentacle, and a horned figure on a throne. The figure of the burning world in the Devil's hand reinforces the idea of hell and damnation. This ideology is often precisely what the seeker fears.

The early Bible never describes Satan as a horned demon. However, a number of pre-Christian traditions honored a "horned one," the lord of the forest. With this statement, I indicate to them a card such as the *Legend Tarot*'s Cernunnos. This provides an opportunity to explain images of the horned forest lord that date back to the Paleolithic age, long prior to the birth of the Christian religion. In an effort to eradicate the old religions, the Church associated its ideas of evil with the old gods, turning them into useful scapegoats. This image reflects the primordial self. With the explanation of the origins of the image, I often show the seeker the Old One from the *Faery Wicca Tarot*, which shadows the Cernunnos figure with an image of the Christos. Nowhere in his teachings did Christ condemn the old ways. He spoke of love. In the Old One card, Christ and Cernunnos both grant blessings. Does this seem an image to fear?

With this new knowledge fresh in mind, I now introduce the core meanings of the Devil card. It is okay to go back to one's base, instinctive nature. But to be strong, we have to move forward from that nature, to harmonize our base desires with positive choices. We can choose to indulge and even overindulge. That is the nature of temptation: too much of a good thing. Do we choose to simply tag along, or do we choose to make wise choices and lead our-selves to a positive, healthy, and stronger outcome?

Fears about the Tower card also come from Biblical traditions rooted in the Tower of Babel story. The story around the Tower of Babel indicates punishment for too much knowledge, for man thinking that he can truly reach God. The outcome of that assump-tion was God sundering both the tower itself and the peoples who built it, scrambling their ability to communicate and hindering their development. This idea of destruction and fury from above is at least strongly implied in the *Quest Tarot* Tower.

Yet, historical research leads to differing thoughts on the origins and purpose of the tower. Babylonian and Mesopotamian cultures coexisted with the ancient Hebrew culture. Excavations of ziggurats document massive towerlike fortresses with cities built on top. Origins of the word Babel likely come from the Akkadian word *babilu,* which means "gate of god." The great ziggurats were fortresses meant to defend a city from invaders. This leads into Vortigern's Fortress, as the Tower card is portrayed in the *Legends Tarot,* as well as The Round Tower from *Faery Wicca.*

Vortigern built his fortress as a refuge from the very Saxons he had hired to fight his battles for him. He built the fortress at Dinas Emrys, as his advisors told him this was the best location. He came to learn quickly that his information was faulty and the fortress would not stand the test of time. His plans were changed, not by his will but by fate. This is the core meaning of the Tower: change; change that you cannot prevent; change that must happen.

The Round Tower card depicts the An Clogas—round stone towers built throughout the Celtic lands for warding off invaders. The tower in this card appears to be standing on unstable land and thus is now breaking apart. The fig-ure in this tower card is willingly jump-ing from the pinnacle, the ghostly outline of wings indicating that he is embracing the chance to fly free and take a chance in the maelstrom. The chance ensures there will be change. He has to take that chance in order to grow. We fear change that we cannot control

The Tower Demolition

The Tower from *The Quest Tarot*

and the Tower card indicates that influence in our lives. Yet without that change we remain stuck and unable to grow. Change helps us embrace and remove our fears. Unexpected changes bring about new challenges and knowledge.

This philosophy of knowledge reflects upon the very nature of a tarot reading. For myself, as a tarot reader, a reading has always been about knowledge, both within and without. My truest work, as a tarot reader, is to help my seekers find the keys to their knowledge, their truths. The more knowledge that I can unlock with them while they sit with me, the more ideas they have to think about in relation to their own lives. Knowledge is power. Gaining knowledge about one's life path, as well as the options and choices along that path, is the true purpose of a good tarot session. In this manner, the tarot is a tool for putting an end to fears and gaining personal empowerment. There is no such thing as too much knowledge. Death, the Devil, and the Tower are not about fear, but about embracing fear and gaining knowledge. May they help cut away the barriers to your journey.

The Celtic Heart Spread

by Valerie Sim

On the way to my daughter's wedding rehearsal dinner, I found myself stuck in traffic. I sat there thinking about the commitment of two souls pledged to each other who wish to travel on a dual journey of discovery and growth. Since I've grown weary of the all-too-prevalent emphasis in tarot readings on questions such as "Does Mikey love me?", "Am I pregnant?", or "When will I meet my soul mate?", I longed for something that would explore how each individual and the relationship itself could grow and blossom. I see the relationship itself as an entity and believe that forgetting that can be a huge mistake.

Since I live and breathe tarot, it is not unusual that, when inspiration strikes, I grab the first piece of paper that comes to hand to record my insight. It was on the back of an ATM withdrawal slip, obtained when I withdrew money for the wedding itself, that I created this spread. I only discovered when I got home that the spread formed a natural heart. I considered that a nod from the universe.

Each person in a relationship needs to grow into him- or herself individually and together, and if they are mutually dedicated to the union and are willing to work on it, the relationship should mature and blossom. That's the premise upon which this spread was based. (Note: The choice of pronouns used throughout is conventional, but by no means judgmental, and this spread works equally well for he/he and she/she relationships.)

Here are the spread positions:

Her

1) Herself
2) Pressing issues, positive and negative
3) What she receives
4) What she gives
5) Personal soul growth necessary for her

Him

6) Himself
7) Pressing issues, positive and negative
8) What he gives
9) What he receives
10) Personal soul growth necessary for him

The Relationship

11) Snapshot of the infant relationship
12) Bond/the karmic tie that binds
13) Lessons for relationship growth
14) Lessons for relationship growth
15) Lessons for relationship growth
16) Blessing for the future (Note: This card can be indicative of a wonderful experience or lesson, or of one that is viewed as negative at the time, but either way it will ultimately be realized as beneficial.)

Sample Reading for Juan and Yolanda

This reading was done as a gift to a couple of soon-to-be-married friends of mine, Juan and Yolanda (names changed to protect their identities). The reading was conducted without charge in exchange for the right to publish the results anonymously.

The cards I drew for Juan and Yolanda from the *Rider-Waite-Smith* deck were as follows:

Yolanda

1) Herself - Six of Wands
2) Pressing issues - Queen of Swords
3) What she receives – Three of Wands

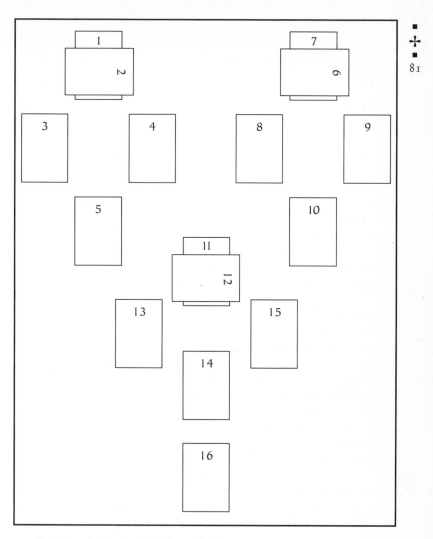

4) What she gives – High Priestess
5) Personal soul growth necessary for her - Eight of Cups

Juan

6) Himself – Two of Pentacles
7) Pressing issues – The Emperor
8) What he gives – Ace of Swords
9) What he receives – The World
10) Personal soul growth necessary for him – Seven of Cups

The Relationship

A Look at the Individuals

This spread is not read in strictly sequential order, but in card groupings. We began by taking an in-depth look at the three entities involved: Yolanda, Juan, and the relationship itself. It is easier to see this if you pretend temporarily that only the three pairs of cards—1 and 2, 6 and 7, and 11 and 12—are in the reading.

We began with Yolanda in cards 1 and 2. Yolanda is painted by the Six of Wands, with the pressing issues being indicated by the Queen of Swords. This is a very passionate woman. She is confident, optimistic, and strong. But her passion is not enough for her. Growing up in a disadvantaged minority family, she realized that she would need more than youth, popularity, and a will to survive. The Queen of Swords has helped her to dedicate herself to her studies, excel in school, and work her way through college. She is understandably proud of her degree. This Queen might also feed into a possible expectation of pain and a tendency to "cut and run" if things don't meet her expectations. Let's see what the rest of the cards have to offer. . . .

Looking at cards 6 and 7, we see that Juan is represented by the Two of Pentacles crossed by the Emperor. This guy knows what it

means to balance one's responsibilities (Two), to play by the rules, and to be an ethical upstanding guy (Emperor). This Two is all about juggling. Considering the appearance of this card, I wasn't surprised to hear that Juan has worked two jobs during most of the past year to save up for their marriage. I think our man is up for the role of husband. He will be able to balance career and family, even if Juan, himself, has concerns about his ability to be the "man of the house."

The relationship itself is indicated by the Six of Cups (snapshot) and the Two of Swords (bond/karmic tie). The Six tells us that the relationship is a haven of peace and fond memories for Juan and Yolanda. It represents emotional enrichment and probably fulfills their earliest memories of what a good relationship should be. The Two, as the bond or karmic tie, represents the necessity of amicably accepting the differences in each other. This is a card of peace of mind, or of making peace. By suspending judgment and by listening to each other's concerns, harmony can be maintained, but there could be a danger of not hearing (or seeing) things that they fear could upset their harmony.

Additionally, for those that believe in past lives, it is easy to interpret the above pair as a conscious choice to reincarnate again together and to work on areas of previous conflict (Two of Swords) after one or more past lives shared (Six of Cups).

I can't help wondering how the Six of Wands and Two of Pentacles will get along with each other. It seems that she might naturally dominate, while he becomes wishy-washy or tries to adjust to her lead. How do her Queen of Swords issues work with his Emperor difficulties? Could she be overly critical and he too concerned about establishing his authority?

Evaluating the Gifts and the Blessing

Next let's move on to look at the gifts (cards 3, 4, 8, 9) and the blessing (card 16) offered by this relationship. How will each support the other? What will be cherished, and what is most important?

With card 4, Yolanda gives to Juan the High Priestess—her gift of ageless feminine wisdom. The High Priestess dwells in the place of knowing, so this card indicates Yolanda's innate understanding of what is really meaningful in life, and a sense of comfort with life's mysteries. She gives to Juan her intuition, her awareness of her greater self, and faith.

In card 3, she receives from her fiancé the gift of the Three of Wands. This is a great sign of cooperation and partnership, of the ability to envision future possibilities. The person in the card stands with his back to us, gazing out to sea, and as Yolanda said spontaneously when viewing this card, "My ship has come in!"

With card 8, Juan gives Yolanda the Ace of Swords. He loves her intellect. This passionate union is not just about sexual attraction.

Juan loves Yolanda's mind. And he gives her his mind, openly and eternally, in exchange. His gift signifies the fact that he honors their ability to communicate and that communication will be important in the long view. This card also shows that Juan will not allow his emotions to cloud his mind, and it reinforces her Queen of the same suit. He gives her his sword. In addition to the Freudian/sexual context, he gives her his loyalty, fight, and stamina, as well as his integrity.

In return, with card 9, he receives from her the World. Ya think? She is his everything and literally "completes" him. But since this is a guy who is indicated by Pentacles and crossed by the Emperor, I don't think his head is in the clouds. He simply knows what he wants, and he has found it.

All four together (it doesn't matter at this point who gave what to whom) we have: Three of Wands, High Priestess (Moon), Ace of Swords, The World (Saturn)—or, written elementally, fire, water, air, earth. All of the elements, and in equal balance!

We could sum it up roughly with this overview: Juan represents that for which Yolanda has been waiting (Three of Wands). She will give to him all that she can of her inner/women's wisdom (High Priestess). In return, he gives her the essence of his thought (Ace Swords), that ideal that he has held in his mind and his heart. He feels, quite simply, that she has given him the world (the World).

Looking to the blessing card (16), we find the Sun. As noted in the introduction to this spread, even had this been a card traditionally regarded as adverse, it would have been something that would eventually be realized as a blessing—but there is no need to stretch to view this card as a blessing. This card in this position is clearly happiness and fulfillment.

Lessons—Advice on Growth

After having looked at the basic energies and interactions of the principals, we need to look at the cards' lessons, or advice on growth, both as individuals and as a couple.

Card 5, that which Yolanda needs to work on, is the Eight of Cups. In the past, when she felt spiritually stifled or unfulfilled she simply moved on. Her challenge here will be to find support in Juan and to not give up on either him, or them, in trying times. (Remember the "cut and run" that I mentioned with the Queen?) She will learn that he can support her inner spirituality and vice versa. Notice that the figure in the card is not walking away from Juan, but rather towards Juan's cards.

Card 10 indicates that Juan needs to work on the Seven of Cups. Okay, so maybe there are a few clouds . . . and appropriately enough there are so many ways we could go with this card. My usual first guess would be self-destructive behavior or delusion, but because of the messages of the other cards, I see this as the many visions he cherishes for providing for the woman he loves and making her happy. Sometimes it is overwhelming and he gets temporarily confused, but he soon gets back on track and uses the Emperor's logic and order to take it one step at a time. (We saw this possibility of wavering earlier in the Two of Pentacles.)

This spread also contains three cards describing lessons/growth as a couple. We will look now at cards 13 (Five of Pentacles), 14 (Ten of Wands), and 15 (Seven of Pentacles). Now we see that even in the Sun-dappled reading above, life intrudes with some hard times that will have to be weathered.

The Five of Pentacles is often interpreted as financial, emotional, or spiritual impoverishment. Ugh! That doesn't sound too good . . . but this is a lesson card, not a dire prediction for the future. We see that Juan and Yolanda may experience some financial difficulties at some point in their relationship, or may feel somehow emotionally shut out. The key is for both to realize that they are not alone! There are two people in this card and they journey together within reach of a haven (the lighted window). As noted in a previous card, the movement is toward the center of the spread. If they pull together they will get beyond this difficulty. Old card interpretations call this the love and relationship card. I have heard Mary K. Greer cite the key phrase, "Good for love, but not for money."

In the Ten of Wands we see a man whose back is straining under his heavy burden. He is literally bent over beneath the load. This card indicates a feeling of being overburdened or of being weighed down by responsibilities. But the sticks are bundled, they are united, so during times like these, by a renewal of their commitment to each other, Juan and Yolanda can work together to share the load. Juan noticed how close the man was to the house, presumably his goal. Once again, they are within sight of a solution.

I often view the Seven of Pentacles as the "is that all there is?" card. I think that's extremely fitting in this case. There often comes a feeling in a relationship, even in a very good one, that one has toiled for little, or that the price has been too steep. Fortunately, by listening to the message of this card, that is a feeling that can be released. It is human to occasionally feel buffeted by life, to get discouraged, or to want to "throw in the towel." As I told Juan and Yolanda, when you feel this way, stop and count your blessings. The man in the card looks defeated, but he has already won! Look at his garden: it is nearly ready to harvest.

The Sun card suggests that things will work out, but Juan and Yolanda will need to periodically evaluate what is most important in their relationship and make adjustments accordingly.

Affirmations

I always finish this spread by having both people create an affirmation based on their personal cards and the blessing card. I print out the three cards with their affirmation and give it to them to take with them in addition to a tape of their reading.

Though they had little or no understanding of the cards before their reading, I am always amazed at how wonderful and appropriate their affirmations are. Here are the affirmations Juan and Yolanda created to cherish their commitment to each other:

Yolanda (cards 1, 2, and 16) "By continuing to love Juan with both my heart and my mind, I will find lasting happiness."

Juan (cards 6, 7, and 16) "By relying on both balance and logic, I will share happiness with Yolanda in the world of our creation."

I couldn't have said it better myself.

Creation Stories
The Gay Tarot
by Lee Bursten

I n February of 2003, Riccardo Minetti, an editor at the Italian tarot publisher Lo Scarabeo, contacted me and asked if I would be interested in creating a gay-themed tarot deck for them. Eighteen months later, the *Gay Tarot*, authored by me and illustrated by Antonella Platano, was published by Lo Scarabeo.

Riccardo's offer was quite unexpected, since I had no experience in creating decks and was not a published tarot author. He had become aware of me through Diane Wilkes's "Tarot Passages" website (www.tarotpassages.com), to which I had contributed many reviews, including reviews of Lo Scarabeo decks, and we had some correspondence regarding certain features of those decks. In one of my reviews I mentioned my sexual orientation in passing, and so when Lo Scarabeo decided to do a gay-themed deck, Riccardo naturally thought of me.

Actually, Lo Scarabeo's initial idea was to do a gay-and-lesbian-themed deck. After the initial surprise and delight in being asked wore off and the project started to coalesce in my mind, I asked if I could approach the deck from a gay male perspective, making it the first all-male tarot deck, gay or straight, released by a major publisher. While there are plenty of woman-centered, feminist, and/or feminine tarot decks, an all-male deck would be something new. I also felt that lesbians have their own story to tell, and that I should stick with what I know.

Riccardo hadn't indicated exactly what kind of gay deck was wanted. Something decorative, perhaps, a highly stylized creation like Lo Scarabeo's *Art Nouveau* deck? Or something erotic, like their *Manara* or *Decameron* decks? Riccardo didn't specify, but I wasn't interested in creating that kind of deck anyway. I wanted to make a deck that I myself would want to read with—a deck without explicit sex or nudity, a warm, encompassing, empowering deck, something that would help gay men develop self-esteem and solidarity in a hostile world. A *Motherpeace* for gay men, if you will.

Fortunately, Lo Scarabeo agreed with my suggestions. Now the time had come to sit down and actually try to imagine what a gay tarot deck would look like. In this regard, I couldn't rely on already-existing decks to guide me. With a few exceptions, most decks that are published nowadays adhere to a particular cultural, ethnic, religious, or historical theme, and the deck author and artist will immediately have the benefit of a pre-existing set of symbols, art styles, clothing, and settings which are automatically suggested by said theme. But homosexuality exists in every culture, every ethnicity, and in every period of history, and thus suggests no particular set of symbols or settings.

Here again, I decided to go with what I knew—that is, my own experiences growing up gay in urban America and trying to lead a "normal" life as a gay man and productive citizen. I also felt it would be appropriate to include diversity of ethnicity, body type, and age. I tend to favor inclusiveness in tarot decks, so, happily, this was in line with my personal preferences.

Then I faced a new dilemma. How could I possibly show themes relating to gay life on all seventy-eight cards? Try as I might, I couldn't imagine doing so without twisting the tarot archetypes into unrecognizable shapes, which would have been contrary to my goal of creating a deck that people would want to read with. In the end, I decided not to attempt to make every card in the deck relate to sex or romantic relationships. After all, most people's lives contain other things besides sex and romance, and I particularly wanted to combat the stereotype that all gay men are obsessed with sex. Therefore, my cards show other aspects of life as well, although always from a gay male perspective.

The next step was to decide what would appear on the Major Arcana cards. This was accomplished by an intuitive process, almost like writing poetry. After I had written descriptions for all twenty-two cards, I went through them all again, discarding several card ideas and replacing them with new ones. For example, my original Hermit showed "an older man with a backpack in a cave. He shines a flashlight down into a pond and illuminates strange and fantastic marine life." This was replaced by an astronaut, orbiting the earth in a spaceship. Likewise, my original Temperance showed a man juggling colored balls (inspired by the *Robin Wood Tarot*'s Temperance). This was replaced with a chef cooking at a stove. Both these choices stemmed from my desire to show men in many different professions (after all, there are gay people in every profession), and both resulted in more creative and interesting interpretations.

I did need to adapt the traditional concepts for some of the Major cards. For the Tower card, for example, I chose a scene in which a young man comes out to his parents, often a time of disruption and stress for all concerned. Another example is the Devil card, which shows a man gazing at a painting of an idealized heterosexual family. The card has been retitled "Self-Hatred."

For the court cards, I settled on a scheme which, for the most part, retains the hierarchical system commonly used in tarot decks. Inspired by James Wanless's *Voyager Tarot* (which uses ranks of Child, Man, Woman, and Sage), I chose Youth, Man, Guide, and Sage as the titles. Obviously, since it's an all-male deck, all the court figures are men. For Queens or Women I substituted Guides, who are winged, angelic males.

Temperance from *The Gay Tarot*

Initially, the numbered Minor cards had me completely stumped. Most modern decks base their scenes for these cards on the *Rider-Waite-Smith* deck, but the job of reinterpreting all those scenes from a gay male perspective seemed overwhelming. I finally found the solution that allowed me to proceed: I would retain the visual composition of the *Rider-Waite-Smith* scenes, but base each card's concept on a facet of the correspondingly numbered Major card. So, for example, the third Major Arcana card, the Empress (here renamed

The Protector from *The Gay Tarot*

"Caretaker" and showing a man with his child, a little girl), embodies themes of child-rearing, and the Three of Cups shows the same man and his child eating ice cream cones in a park, under a statue of three women dancing, thus establishing a visual connection to the traditional scene.

For some cards I had to loosen the constraints of this system a bit, mostly because, for certain numbered Minors, I wanted the images to specifically comment on the *Rider-Waite-Smith* deck designs. For example, the *RWS* Three of Swords shows a heart impaled by three swords. Given my modern, urban setting, I thought it would be perfect to show three broken umbrellas lying across each other on a rainy sidewalk, in the same pattern as the three *RWS* swords. Now, on the face of it, this doesn't seem to relate to the child-rearing theme established by the third Major card, the Caretaker. However, feelings of heartbreak and betrayal can certainly arise between parents and children, especially when we remember Shakespeare's famous line, "How sharper than a serpent's tooth it is / To have a thankless child!" And in a more political context, this sadness and heartbreak can also refer to the difficulties faced in our society by gay people who want to adopt children (or who want to be permitted to raise their own children).

After completing the card descriptions, I sent them off to Riccardo. Soon after that, Riccardo told me they had chosen an artist: Antonella Platano, well-known in Italy for her comic book art. He sent me some sample cards she had done, and I gave my wholehearted approval. Riccardo proceeded to translate my card descriptions into Italian for Antonella, which must have been quite a job.

Meanwhile, I got to work on my last remaining task, which was to write the "little white booklet" (LWB) that would be included with the deck. I have often found LWBs to be rather obscure when it comes to explaining the imagery on the Minor Arcana, and so, in the limited space available, I gave each Minor card a short title that explains the action being shown on the card, and then a list of pos-

sible divinatory meanings, so that the reader has a basic understanding of my intent for each card.

After sending the LWB to Lo Scarabeo, my work was essentially
done. Lo Scarabeo graciously asked for my input regarding a few
matters, such as the choice of card image for the outer box. I was
quite pleased when I saw the final box design, which included two
of the more politically outspoken cards on the back and sides.
Riccardo sent me scans of the Majors when they were completed,
and then of the entire deck when it was done. I cannot describe
how immensely satisfying and exciting it was to see my ideas take
physical form under the pen of a talented artist like Antonella. Then
it was simply a matter of waiting for the deck to be printed and dis-
tributed. Words can't express my feelings of excitement and pride
when I held the printed deck in my hands for the first time, and
again when I saw the deck on the shelf at my local bookstore.

Gay Tarot in a Straight World

I've referred a few times to a gay male perspective or sensibility. But
what do these words really mean? I certainly don't believe that there is
one particular gay male sensibility; in fact, such an assertion would
reinforce rather than dispel the stereotypes that unfortunately are so
prevalent in our society. It may be easier for me to say what I don't
mean. I don't mean the kind of gay sensibility one finds in depictions
of gay people in the popular media. For example, I enjoy watching
Showtime's *Queer as Folk* television series, but I don't live like those
characters, and in fact I suspect the majority of gay people don't
either. And I'm not being judgmental about those who do. I simply
wanted to make a tarot deck that reflected the kind person I am, rather
than the exotic creatures one often sees in film and television.

I suppose what I mean by "gay viewpoint" or "gay sensibility" is
a congruity of interests based on shared experiences. For example,
when a gay person (or a member of any oppressed minority) sees
the Justice card, which illustrates the unhappy experiences that
many gay people in our society have suffered at the hands of the
justice system, he or she may experience a feeling of recognition
and immediate understanding. Other cards that take an outspo-
kenly political stand include trump XX, Beyond Judgment, which
shows a gay rights parade; and the Ten of Cups, which echoes the
standard scene of a man and a woman gazing at a rainbow with
two children dancing nearby, except that in the *Gay Tarot* the man
and woman are replaced by two men.

Of course, I'm hoping others besides gay men will use this deck as well. Lesbian, bisexual, transgendered, and straight people might all find reasons to investigate the *Gay Tarot*, both because they can use it to read for gay men, and also because it could be an interesting and nonthreatening way to investigate issues of sexual and gender diversity.

Some might ask whether a gay tarot deck is even a valid concept, or if it's just an attempt to impose a "politically correct" viewpoint on the tarot. I won't pretend to be able to answer this question. I tend to approach things in a practical, down-to-earth, common-sense manner. The fact of the matter is, there are cultural and ethnic theme decks, there are woman-centered decks. I see no reason why the gay male experience can't be reflected in a tarot deck as well; after all, one can easily find novels, plays, and films that are directed towards a gay male audience. Perhaps in a perfect world it wouldn't occur to anyone to create works of art that separate out gay people from straight people, or any one group from another. But some would say that a perfect world would be one where people could feel free to celebrate their identities, whether ethnic, cultural, or sexual. I like to think of the *Gay Tarot* as my small way of contributing to that celebration, of throwing my hat into the air, à la Mary Tyler Moore, to celebrate the gay male spirit.

The Karmic Insight Spread

by Christine Jette

The law of karma comes from Buddhist doctrine and is related to reincarnation. It teaches that every thought and deed must eventually create its own effects, for good or ill, which then must be endured or enjoyed by the individual involved. Karma is carried from one life to the next and worked out (repaid) over eons of time until enlightenment occurs and there is no further debt. In its more elaborate form, karma maintains the balance of cosmic debt. It is important to note here, however, that Western ideas about judgment are foreign to the Eastern philosophy that originally produced karmic theory.

On the individual level, as well as the universal, the law of karma is the principle of adjustment, balance, equilibrium, and harmony on all levels of being. It gives back to each person the actual consequences of an act, wisely adjusting each effect to its cause wherever disturbances occur. Its action is perceivable, and it is the law of readjustment that restores equilibrium to the broken harmony of the world. Karma is not based on spiteful punishment, but an all-wise equilibrium that searches for the highest good and a compassionate restoration of order.

Déjà Vu: Past, Present, and Future Lives

Have you ever been meditating and remembered being another person in another time? What about the time you went to a place you had never been before only to be overwhelmed with the sensation of familiarity? Or, perhaps in deep-work therapy, you experience traumas from this lifetime, and suddenly find yourself reliving traumas from another lifetime. The term "past life" is used to define such experiences, but I believe the phrase is limited because time is not linear and space has more than three dimensions. Mystic Edgar Cayce and physicist Albert Einstein agreed that all things of the past and future exist now, somehow interwoven into a complex reality. Einstein called it the time-space continuum; Cayce referred to it as a multidimensional reality.

Mystic Jane Roberts, best known for her "Seth" books, believed that all our past and future lives are being lived now, each in its own dimension, as part of a greater soul or greater being. According to Roberts, we can penetrate into these other dimensions, or lives, to bring knowledge and understanding for transformation. By doing this, our present life can transform our other lives. Or, to put it another way, how we live now, in this life, affects both our past and future lives; we create our own reality in this life by our beliefs and desires. Of course, getting in touch with our beliefs and desires is where the tarot cards come in handy.

Before You Begin . . .

Working with past lives is effective when the transformation process is the main objective. Past-life work is not play and should not be used to boost the ego. We all would like to have been a great leader, or the king or queen of something in a past life, rather than a common village peasant. This is not at all the point.

Experiencing past-life memories can free us from problems or challenges that now hold us back from attaining our greatest potential or completing our life's work. Problems related to past-life issues correlate to what we are dealing with in the present life, but past-life memories can be tricky. We need to be careful and not use a past-life issue as

an excuse for negative behavior in this life. We run the risk of mis-
using the past-life connection and heaping up more karma if we
blame someone for our negative feelings, give ourselves permission
to behave in an antisocial way, or falsely elevate our past-life status.

For example, you don't like your current boss, so in your fantasy
past life you were in charge. Most of the time, whatever problems
we have now we had then—but they may not be as bad now
because we have learned a few things in our ensuing lives. Our job
is to see a useful connection between past and present and apply
that knowledge with sensitivity to help heal this life's problems. By
so doing, we create a better future.

Past-life material is often painful and is best avoided if you are
not ready. Timing is everything, and the best results occur when
the process is natural and unforced. Please seek professional counseling if you need support. Refer to the professional practice section below for suggestions on working with the past lives of clients.

The Karmic Insight Layout

The purpose of the Karmic Insight spread is to clarify the lessons,
purposes, and goals of this lifetime. It also looks at unresolved
past-life issues that are in the forefront of this life, and illuminates
your struggles through tarot in a constructive, life-affirming way.

I have chosen nine cards because nine represents integration of
experiences, self-awareness, and maturity. It is also the number of
fate, luck, capability, and magic. I have placed the cards in a circle
because time is not linear and we are all connected, life without
end. The circle starts at the bottom to represent the past, continues
clockwise to symbolize the forward motion of our lives, yet ends
where it begins because the future is built on the past. The Karma
card is at the center and radiates outward because it symbolizes
our soul's journey through all lifetimes—past, present, and future.

You will notice several descriptions (possible meanings) after
some of the positions. Don't expect to answer each one. Select the
issue that jumps out at you, the one that feels right or makes the
most sense now. Then trust that your intuition is leading you where
you need to go for your highest good—because it is.

Many times we meet people and have the feeling that we know
them from before. We feel connected to them in ways that are difficult to describe yet feel real to us. We may find that we like the
same things, or catch glimpses of past-life experiences together.
Sometimes, a full-blown past-life memory will surface.

Two people who feel connected by a past life can do this spread at the same time, using two different decks. If either of you gets the same card in the same position, the predominance of the same suit, or a similar number of Major Arcana cards, interpret it as a sign of past-life connections with this person. If the cards seem totally unrelated, you might ask yourself what gifts you have to give one another, or what you have to learn from one another in this lifetime. Only you can decide if you have had a past experience with this person, but you are together in this life for a reason. What is it?

Shuffle the cards and select one card, facedown, for each of the nine positions below. Take a few deep breaths. When you are ready, turn the cards over and take note of your immediate, uncensored reaction to the cards as a whole. This is an overview of your life—past, present, and future—in picture form. How do you feel about the artwork?

Cards 1, 2, and 3: The Past

Card 1: What you know and keep repeating from other lifetimes. This is your basic approach to all lives, your outlook. For example, are you emotional, rational, sensitive, creative, etc.? This card represents who you know yourself to be.

Card 2: Blocks from past lives, challenges. Where have you stumbled in the past? It points to areas in this life that continue to be problematic.

Card 3: Strengths from past lives, the lessons learned well. What has made you strong through all lifetimes? This card represents growth that you carry over to the present.

Cards 4, 5, and 6: The Present

Card 4: What are you here to learn this time? What are your current challenges or life lessons? If you learn your lessons well, this card represents the wisdom you will gain. Think of it as a card of great opportunity—no pain, no gain.

Card 5: Blocks from this lifetime. Stuck places that never seem to change even though you have done a lot of spiritual work. You may have strong, painful, fearful, or angry feelings attached to this card. If so, respect the work and know that you are doing the best you can. Consider, too, that you are exactly where you need to be for your soul's development. Stop the reading if you are too uncomfortable, or seek professional advice. You do not have to do this alone.

Card 6: Connecting present-life issues to past-life experience.

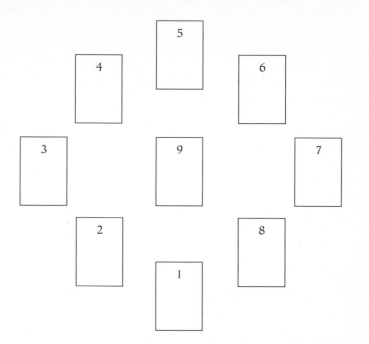

How is the block in this lifetime related to those in other lifetimes? What purpose does it serve? Look for a relationship between this card and Card 2, blocks from past lives. Taken together, what story do they tell?

Cards 7, 8, and 9: The Future

Card 7: Action to take for healing and soul development. What would happen if you did this? How would you feel? This action may not be appropriate if you are not ready. Seek outside advice if you need it.

Card 8: The lessons learned and wisdom gained. Your strengths and what you need for the fullest expression of your soul's development through all lifetimes.

Card 9: Karma. Your future direction and where you go from here, the next step on your journey. This card represents your next incarnation and is the link to your past, present, and future. It gives you a glimpse of the bigger picture against an eternal backdrop. What is the ongoing theme of all your lifetimes? How are they related? Can you now sense an overriding purpose or meaning to your life? If so, what is it?

Putting It All Together

I believe it is the relationship of the cards to one another that yields the most useful information. Look at the spread up and down, across, and diagonally to see how cards relate and interact with one another. For example, look at cards 1, 5, and 9: How can you put what you know (the past, card 1) to good use today (the present block, card 5), in order to create your own karma tomorrow (card 9, building a better future)? Where are the compatibilities or conflicts in the cards? What story do they weave?

It may help to make an entry in your tarot journal. You can also leave the cards out for a while, meditate, or program a dream for more insight. Trust your intuition. Only you can decide the personal value of the layout.

If you need more information, draw another card from the same deck and place it under the position in question as the "Advice or Summary Card"—that is, ask for specific instructions on what to do or study next. Any card associated with the unconscious, emotions, the psyche, or karma is a strong indicator of a past-life experience. Of special importance are the High Priestess, the Moon, Judgment (the karma card), and any Cup.

If you pull advice or summary cards, Wands frequently mean sex, passion, or the energy to create, Pentacles imply how much "work" is required in a relationship or situation, or describe money issues; Cups refer to love and emotions; Swords point to conflict and decisions; court cards indicate your stage of development, self-image, or the people you bring into your life for life lessons; and the Major Arcana signify karma and spiritual lessons.

For another perspective, try Llewellyn's Special Topics in Tarot Series and start with *Past-Life and Karmic Tarot* (2004) by Edain McCoy. I created this layout without knowledge of McCoy's book, so I am interested in how we compare and contrast. Feel free to e-mail me and let me know: Findingthemuse@aol.com.

Above all, remember that nothing in tarot is preordained and we are not puppets on a string. Tarot card energies themselves are neutral energies; there is no "good" card vs. "bad" card. Tarot cards symbolize our life situations. No tarot-card configuration is out to destroy us, because there is something valuable to learn in every situation, however painful or conflicted. It is up to us to search for the meaning. It is how we apply the energies in force that makes all the difference.

For example, I groan every time the Sun comes up in one of my readings, and I get it a lot. I do not like that card! In my life, the Sun represents burnout or sunburn—laying waste to the desert. I feel overpowered by its rays and I get depressed in the summer. To most people the Sun means happiness, success, playfulness, or attainment—the nourishment required for fertile fields. The energy of the Sun is the same, whether sunburn or suntan. The difference is perception. Or, according to Jane Roberts and Seth, we create our own reality through our beliefs and desires.

If we've been using a situation in a specific way that creates destructive energy, we always have the choice of using the same energy in a more positive, constructive way—even if only through a change in outlook or attitude. The tarot is a symbolic roadmap, but, just like the stars of astrology, the cards impel, they do not compel. You still retain your power of personal choice as the author of your own karmic life.

Professional Practice

The past-life spread can be used as a specialized reading on its own or in combination with other services such as healing touch or hypnotherapy. I often combine a therapeutic touch treatment with a tarot reading. In my work with past-life issues, I have discovered a few precautions and I pass them on to you to do with as you will. (This is just one woman's take on the subject, after all.)

Based on my observations, past-life traumas often underlie the chronic, present-day problems that are difficult to resolve. One role of the healer is to help connect present-life issues to past-life experiences. Think of past-life work in terms of layers, starting with the present and working backward through time. I believe that past-life work should first address the blocks from this lifetime. This starts the healing process and allows traumas from other lifetimes to bubble to the surface for discovery, one layer at a time. The healer then helps the client relate past-life work to present-life situations, so that the entire trauma is eventually released.

The timing of discovery is important. When past-life information is discovered at the right moment, it will help the person understand himself better and increase feelings of self-love. If it is forced, or done at the wrong time, it can increase a person's negativity toward self or others. It is never good practice to expose your client to past-life information when she or he is not ready for it. The healing of old wounds has its own timetable of letting go. It is not for us to decide.

When doing past-life readings, be prepared for your client's strong feelings, such as pain, anger, or fear. Learn to listen well. Compassion takes many forms, and sometimes just "being there" in the present moment of pain is all you can do. You may also need to stop the reading, or suggest professional counseling. You can find information on how to make referrals in my book *Professional Tarot* (Llewellyn 2003).

Always remember that the purpose of past-life work is healing and soul development. Past-life issues are related to the tasks our clients have undertaken in this lifetime and what they need to do in order to grow. As professional readers, it is not our job to "fix it." We are working in a person's sacred space. It is important that we respect the power of the work. We learn to respect the humility of our position as professional readers in the grand scheme of the universe, and focus on unconditional love—the greatest healer of all.

Teaching Tarot

by Corrine Kenner

You can share your love of the tarot—and learn more about the cards yourself—by teaching a tarot class. You don't need to be a Grand High Poobah of the Esoteric Arts in order to teach tarot. You simply need to be willing to share what you know with others.

Of course, you should know the cards well. You should understand the basic structure and the symbolism of the deck, and you should be able to explain how you put it to use. You should also be intimately familiar with the cards in your favorite tarot deck. You should be able to see each of them in your mind's eye. You should know what each card means by itself, and what it means in combination with other cards.

You should also know what you don't know—so that you can refer your students to other sources of information. I usually keep a comprehensive tarot text and a good symbol dictionary nearby when I teach, because I have learned that students will inevitably come up with questions that I can't answer off the top of my head. (I've also learned that I can sometimes blank out and struggle with easy questions, if someone lobs a softball at me that I don't expect.) In a field like tarot, obscure references and associations are bound to come up during discussions—but those oddball questions and conversations are some of the most unexpected delights of teaching a tarot class.

In fact, decide right now that you won't be embarrassed if you can't answer every question, even with a reference book at hand. Most students will probably be far more forgiving than you expect if you tell them you don't know all the answers—and researching a few mysteries could even be a bonding experience for your group. After all, people who sign up for a tarot class are generally self-motivated adults, who simply want to learn what you know.

Do you feel more confident yet? Good. You're ready to teach.

Before you can get started, you will need to find a space for your classes to meet. There are any number of possibilities:

- You can hold classes in your own living room or around your dining room table, if you feel comfortable letting members of the public into your home.

- You might also look into reserving space at a public library or community center, which generally offer meeting rooms free or at a nominal cost.

- Some businesses have meeting rooms that they are willing to lend or rent out after hours. Many restaurants and coffee shops, for example, are happy to host meetings and groups—especially during off-peak hours—because participants will inevitably order drinks and desserts.

- You may be able to offer a class through the continuing education office at a nearby college. Simply write them a short proposal that reads like an ad for your class, and summarize your credentials. If you want your classes to appeal to the largest number of prospective students, emphasize tarot as a method of self-development and as an introduction to the study of symbolism, art, and mythology.

- Most bookstore owners and specialty shop managers are eager to host speakers and seminars that relate to the merchandise they sell. If you want to go commercial, simply dress professionally, visit the store in person, and ask to see the manager or events coordinator. Bring along an outline of your class schedule—and be sure to prepare a list of tarot decks and books that you are willing to recommend to your students.

Whatever facility you choose should have ample parking, as well as accessible bathroom accommodations. It should be cen-

trally located and easy to find. Of course, you will get calls asking
for directions. You may want to write those directions down ahead
of time, so you can give them out over the phone.

Naturally, your meeting space should include plenty of room for
your students to sit, spread their cards, and practice reading—but
that doesn't mean everyone needs a chair. In tarot classes, I have
found that many people actually prefer to sit on the floor, where
they will have plenty of room to work. Just make sure you do have
some chairs and table space available for those who want it.

Once you know where you will meet, set your schedule. Many
tarot classes meet weekly for four to six weeks. More focused workshops usually meet just once. Be sure to check your calendar: try to
avoid classes that meet close to holidays, when many prospective
students might be traveling or with their families.

Then set your fee. If you are teaching through a college, admin-
istrators will determine the price and pay you according to their set
standards. A bookstore will usually pay you a standard stipend, in
order to be able to offer the class to their customers for free. If you
are teaching on your own, set your prices in line with other continuing education classes in your area. Generally speaking, each class
should cost about the same as comparable "entertainment," such
as the price of popcorn and a movie in your area.

Next, publicize your class. Write an announcement, and mail,
fax, or e-mail it to local newspapers, radio stations, and television
stations. Your message can be short, like this: "Jane Doe will teach
a four-week Introduction to Tarot class beginning at 7 p.m., Wednesday, October 24, at the Parkview Community Center in Hilldale.
Registration is $45. For more information, call (123) 456-7890, or

e-mail jane@janedoe.com." Also, make a flyer, and post copies in places where your prospective students are likely to see it: grocery stores, book stores, gas stations, and coffee shops usually have public bulletin boards. According to some experts, flyers with red borders get the most notice. Posters with tear-off tabs also give people an easy way to follow up if they are interested.

Once you have the logistics in place, determine exactly what material you will cover in your classes. Think back to the information you wanted to learn when you first discovered the tarot. You'll want to go over each of the Major Arcana cards, of course, as well as the symbolism and structure of the four suits. You might want to teach by demonstrating your own techniques, or by asking everyone in the group to read and discuss the same book, such as Anthony Louis's *Tarot Plain and Simple* or Joan Bunning's *Learning the Tarot*. You can also find sample class outlines in Christine Jette's *Professional Tarot: The Business of Reading, Consulting & Teaching*.

As you organize the material you plan to teach, visualize the handouts you will need to prepare. Most people appreciate a few "cheat sheets" with suggested meanings for each card, as well as diagrams of well-known spreads and layouts. You don't need to get all of your materials ready before your first class, however; leave some room to change and adapt to the needs of your class.

If you are teaching a class for beginners, I strongly encourage you to make sure all of your students use the same deck, such as the *The Robin Wood Tarot* or the *Universal Tarot*. At the first class I taught, hardly anyone was working with the same deck. I spent a lot of time answering questions about subtle variations in the cards, like "What does *my* Fool card mean?", "Why doesn't my Queen of Wands have a cat?", and "Why do all of her cards have Roman numerals?" If you want to compare decks, use cards from your own collection, so that you can control the flow of discussion.

As you plan each class, remember to build in time for your students to practice their new skills with each other. Group readings and collective spreads are always popular, because they give students a chance to offer their own interpretations of each card—and in tarot, students learn as much from each other as they learn from a teacher.

Also, schedule a break or two—especially if your classes last more than ninety minutes. You may want to make sure that coffee, tea, or snacks are available.

When your class meets for the first time, take a few minutes so that everyone can get to know each other. Go around the room and ask all of your students to introduce themselves. Ask each member of the class what they hope to learn—and take notes, so you'll remember.

Then take a deep breath, smile, and start teaching.

A Closer Look At:

The Quest Tarot

Created and illustrated by Joseph Ernest Martin

- 79 full-color cards and a 312-page illustrated book, *The Compass*

- Cards are 4¾ x 2¾, with reversible backs and illustrated pips

- Card imagery uses advanced three-dimensional computer modeling for a fresh, contemporary look

- Each card is marked with the corresponding astrological symbols, Hebrew letters, and runes

- Illustrated companion book presents new ways to work with the deck, including methods for spelling out names and phrases and creating spreads with detailed timelines

Zapped!
When Clients Explode

by Elizabeth Hazel

Once upon a time, when I was a young sprig of a tarotist, I signed up to read at a large two-day New Age convention, one of the first of its kind in this region. It was held in a monstrous arena, with hundreds of booths for vendors, readers, massage therapists, aura photographers, and the like. Thousands of people attended the event. The noise was incredible, and it was not the best setting for giving good tarot readings. Nevertheless, I persisted, and did pretty well on the first day.

On the second day, I was exhausted. The setting was draining my energies by the hour. Still, I felt committed to getting through the second day of tarot readings before making the long drive home. In the afternoon, a young woman sat down at my table for a reading. She was foreign, and her mother accompanied her to translate. This added a complication, but having previously worked with translators, I was willing to try. I focused and centered, had the woman shuffle the deck, and proceeded to lay out the cards.

Her reading was an unqualified mess. The young woman's life was beset by a devastating romantic failure. I worked my way through the cards gently and diplomatically, sensing that she was fairly upset. At the point where I noted that the man had left her, she exploded into screams and tears, all in a foreign language. The weak psychic shield I'd managed to erect was shattered, and I felt like I'd been physically assaulted and psychically zapped.

I appealed to her mother for help. The client would not be calmed, and was disrupting readings in nearby booths. Finally her mother got her up and walked her out of the area. My nerves were shot to hell, and I was ruined for more readings. After returning home, I made a point of discussing the incident with more experienced readers, who gave me very good advice. Now I'm passing it along to you. If you're a new reader, or even an experienced reader who hasn't had a client go ballistic during a reading, listen and learn!

Reading when you're tired is dangerous. If your energies are tapped, you can be zapped. The best readings flow when the reader is grounded and surrounded by protective energy. This preparation allows you to be completely open to the client. If you're too tired to ground and surround, a twitchy client can be a disaster. Your open "eye" is a huge gaping target. Learn your limits! If you get tired after ten readings, then stop and take a break. No one is keeping score. If you sign up for a two-day event, schedule break times so you can rest and recharge your energies.

Big public events are not for every reader, as they require concentration in spite of traffic noise and other reader's vibes. While participating in events is a good way to develop a clientele, it is also the most difficult venue for giving readings. Prepare in advance for this additional stress. Get a good night's sleep, have a protective crystal on hand, put salt in your pocket and shoes, or spend the week preceding the event meditating and developing a heavy-duty psychic shield.

Exploding clients aren't mad at you, they're mad at life. Don't take an explosion personally. If you're in a private setting, it is okay to allow the client to vent for a few minutes. Keep tissues handy. People cry, sob, moan, and react to readings that touch their hearts or step on their last nerves. That's perfectly acceptable. Screaming and violent emoting, however, need to be nipped in the bud. If a client is having a rough time during the reading, take a pause to reground and re-shield. Trust me, she won't notice, and it is necessary to gain emotional distance for coping compassionately yet firmly, and to make good judgments about what happens next. In a private setting, you have more flexibility, and can direct the reading after the client has regained her composure.

Identify the cause or source of the emotional outburst. Give the client a few moments to explain why he is so upset. Let him express his disappointment, frustration, or anger. This is a difficult but enormously helpful service for the client, as you are allowing him to cleanse and release the source of his pain. Do not to allow this to continue for too long. If he starts to repeat his complaints, then it is time to shift the focus of the reading. If he wants to continue venting, remind him that the reading has a time limit, and you want him to receive whatever assistance is available in the time remaining. Your ability to resume command at this point is critical. The client's venting provides clues to target your questions and remarks.

Redirect the reading into proactive dialogue. Guide the client with questions about her best options for the future. In my experience, the clients most likely to cry or vent are ones who have ended a painful relationship, or who have been abandoned by a significant other. Helpful questions might include: What are your best sources of support? Do you have a network of supportive friends or family you can spend time with? What can you do for yourself that the relationship prevented you from doing? Are there ways you can give of yourself to others? (Sometimes helping others takes away the sting of loss.) Is there a project you can do; are you interested in taking a class; do you belong to a special interest group? Identify activities that offer positive outlets unrelated to the cause of sorrow. Reassure the client that she can move her life in a positive direction in the future. Have the client draw an additional card from the deck to represent the best possible way for healing her hurt.

Most readers are deeply sympathetic, and will be very hurt by the client's distress. It might be a struggle to resume the reading, even in a private setting. You can offer to end the reading and continue another day if the client's distress is extreme or frightening in its intensity. If the client is not trying to regain his composure, then end the reading. Base your charges on the time he has taken. If the reading is cut short, prorate your normal fee to reflect this.

If the client chooses to continue the reading, a professional demeanor is a must. The fact that a client has exploded proves she is in desperate need of the sympathy of an unbiased listener. But it is also a warning that she might need more than you can give her with a tarot reading. You may choose to offer a referral to a therapist or help group if the client is open to this kind of suggestion.

It is up to the tarotist to enforce the boundaries of appropriateness. Your time is valuable. If the time limit passes, make the client aware of the costs of additional time. I give this reminder not as a testament to greed but as a reinforcement of respect. A client on an emotional rampage (for whatever reason) must be reminded that he contracted you for professional services. If the client isn't respectful of your time and limits, then he won't respect your advice either.

If you are in a public setting like a psychic fair or convention, your options are much more limited. You have to respond smoothly and quickly. Believe me, this is tough! Your own sympathy works against you, especially if you weren't expecting the outburst. The more quickly you can return to "professional" mode, the better off you'll be in resolving the situation with the client. The most effective technique to remember in this situation is:

Stand up and move away from the table. By physically removing yourself from the table, you've distanced yourself from the client. This gives you a moment to do some quick thinking; and on a subconscious level, your body language conveys a message to the client. If you can, quietly move behind the client and place your hand on her shoulder or neck, and bend down to whisper that she needs to go to a more private area. Because violently emoting clients disrupts other readers, it is critical to move them out of the area immediately. At a small event, there might be scheduling assistants who can help. Once you've stood up, you can signal them that you need help. If the client is screaming, an experienced event worker will already be moving to intervene.

At a large event like a convention, you'll probably be on your own, and getting dirty looks from nearby readers. It is imperative to be firm with the client. Help him stand and walk away from the area. If the client resists, you can quietly explain that he is interrupting other people's readings. Escort him to a rest room or uninhabited hallway. If he has attended the event with friends or relatives, return the client to them, and offer a brief explanation of what happened.

Readings are of short duration at psychic events—usually fifteen or twenty minutes. Doing the math, if a client explodes halfway through the reading, you only have seven or ten minutes to do damage control. This is not going to cut the mustard in a worst-case scenario. Solicit help from event workers or the client's companions. Accept that the reading is at an end. If you've already been paid, keep it: you've earned it. If the client hasn't paid, forget it.

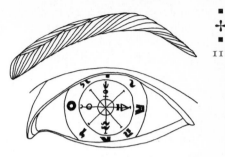

Although it might seem like selfish advice, it is important to take care of yourself after this kind of explosion. Do not try to console an exploding client alone if you can quietly, quickly, and efficiently obtain assistance from others. Other people are affected by an exploding client, including neighboring readers and their clients, as well as any clients you are scheduled to read for during the remainder of the event.

Some readers will never have to cope with an exploding client, and I sincerely hope that you never do! In retrospect, my client exploded because I was tired and unobservant, and did not take into consideration the cultural norms of a foreign client. In her culture, her reaction might have been expected as a signal of sincere remorse. This is not a blanket warning against reading for people from other cultures, but more of an admonition to work with foreign clients with additional sensitivity.

It is preferable to prevent a client from exploding in the first place. Observe the overall demeanor of a client when she sits down for a reading. If she seems uncommonly nervous or stressed, or has a desperate look in her eyes, read those body-language signals as warnings. Before starting the reading, ask the client to do some deep breathing to gain calm and focus. Continue to watch the client's body language and eyes for any sign that emotions could be erupting to the surface. Gauge responses to statements you make about the cards with repeated eye contact. Slow the pace or stop if you see signs of traumatic upset on the client's face; inquire if she needs a break or a breather.

An exploding client tests the limits of a reader's sympathy and professionalism. But with vigilant observation and tactful inquiry, the situation need never occur. Professional readers should have their own "in case of emergency" list to refer to when clients do unexpected or upsetting things. If you are beginning your journey as a tarot counselor, spend some time planning what you would do if confronted with an extreme situation.

The Wheel

2006 *Almanac*

1 Sunday

Moon in Capricorn
Moon enters Aquarius 7:14 am

New Year's Day ♦ Kwanzaa ends

2 Monday

Moon in Aquarius

Hanukkah ends

3 Tuesday

Moon in Aquarius
Moon enters Pisces 7:43 am

4 Wednesday

Moon in Pisces

5 Thursday

Moon in Pisces
Moon enters Aries 9:44 am

6 Friday

Moon in Aries
Second quarter 1:56 pm

7 Saturday

Moon in Aries
Moon enters Taurus 2:09 pm

8 Sunday
Moon in Taurus

9 Monday
Moon in Taurus
Moon enters Gemini 8:58 pm

10 Tuesday
Moon in Gemini

11 Wednesday
Moon in Gemini

12 Thursday
Moon in Gemini
Moon enters Cancer 5:50 am

13 Friday
Moon in Cancer

14 Saturday
Moon in Cancer
Full Moon 4:48 am
Moon enters Leo 4:31 pm

15 Sunday
Moon in Leo

16 Monday
Moon in Leo

Birthday of Martin Luther King, Jr. (observed)

17 Tuesday
Moon in Leo
Moon enters Virgo 4:49 am

18 Wednesday
Moon in Virgo

19 Thursday
Moon in Virgo
Moon enters Libra 5:49 pm

20 Friday
Moon in Libra
Sun enters Aquarius 12:15 am

21 Saturday
Moon in Libra

22 Sunday

Moon in Libra
Moon enters Scorpio 5:28 am
Fourth Quarter 10:14 am

23 Monday

Moon in Scorpio

24 Tuesday

Moon in Scorpio
Moon enters Sagittarius 1:38 pm

25 Wednesday

Moon in Sagittarius

26 Thursday

Moon in Sagittarius
Moon enters Capricorn 5:31 pm

27 Friday

Moon in Capricorn

28 Saturday

Moon in Capricorn
Moon enters Aquarius 6:09 pm

29 Sunday
Moon in Aquarius
New Moon 9:15 am

Chinese New Year (dog)

30 Monday
Moon in Aquarius
Moon enters Pisces 5:32 pm

31 Tuesday
Moon in Pisces

Islamic New Year

1 Wednesday
Moon in Pisces
Moon enters Aries 5:46 pm

2 Thursday
Moon in Aries

Imbolc ✦ Groundhog Day

3 Friday
Moon in Aries
Moon enters Taurus 8:31 pm

4 Saturday
Moon in Taurus

5 Sunday
Moon in Taurus
Second Quarter 1:29 am

6 Monday
Moon in Taurus
Moon enters Gemini 2:32 am

7 Tuesday
Moon in Gemini

8 Wednesday
Moon in Gemini
Moon enters Cancer 11:33 am

9 Thursday
Moon in Cancer

10 Friday
Moon in Cancer
Moon enters Leo 10:44 pm

11 Saturday
Moon in Leo

12 Sunday

Moon in Leo
Full Moon 11:44 pm

13 Monday

Moon in Leo
Moon enters Virgo 11:13 am

14 Tuesday

Moon in Virgo

Valentine's Day

15 Wednesday

Moon in Virgo

16 Thursday

Moon in Virgo
Moon enters Libra 12:09 am

17 Friday

Moon in Libra

18 Saturday

Moon in Libra
Moon enters Scorpio 12:11 pm
Sun enters Pisces 2:25 pm

19 Sunday
Moon in Scorpio

20 Monday
Moon in Scorpio
Moon enters Sagittarius 9:38 pm

Presidents' Day (observed)

21 Tuesday
Moon in Sagittarius
Fourth Quarter 2:17 am

22 Wednesday
Moon in Sagittarius

23 Thursday
Moon in Sagittarius
Moon enters Capricorn 3:16 am

24 Friday
Moon in Capricorn

25 Saturday
Moon in Capricorn
Moon enters Aquarius 5:14 am

26 Sunday
Moon in Aquarius

27 Monday
Moon in Aquarius
Moon enters Pisces 4:56 am
New Moon 7:31 pm

28 Tuesday
Moon in Pisces

Mardi Gras

1 Wednesday
Moon in Pisces
Moon enters Aries 4:18 am

Ash Wednesday

2 Thursday
Moon in Aries

3 Friday
Moon in Aries
Moon enters Taurus 5:22 am

4 Saturday
Moon in Taurus

5 Sunday

Moon in Taurus
Moon enters Gemini 9:37 am

6 Monday

Moon in Gemini
Second Quarter 3:16 pm

7 Tuesday

Moon in Gemini
Moon enters Cancer 5:38 pm

8 Wednesday

Moon in Cancer

9 Thursday

Moon in Cancer

10 Friday

Moon in Cancer
Moon enters Leo 4:42 am

11 Saturday

Moon in Leo

12 Sunday
Moon in Leo
Moon enters Virgo 5:23 pm

13 Monday
Moon in Virgo

14 Tuesday
Moon in Virgo
Full Moon 6:35 pm

Purim

15 Wednesday
Moon in Virgo
Moon enters Libra 6:12 am

16 Thursday
Moon in Libra

17 Friday
Moon in Libra
Moon enters Scorpio 5:59 pm

St. Patrick's Day

18 Saturday
Moon in Scorpio

19 Sunday
Moon in Scorpio

20 Monday
Moon in Scorpio
Moon enters Sagittarius 3:43 am
Sun enters Aries 1:25 pm

Ostara

21 Tuesday
Moon in Sagittarius

22 Wednesday
Moon in Sagittarius
Moon enters Capricorn 10:36 am
Fourth Quarter 2:10 pm

23 Thursday
Moon in Capricorn

24 Friday
Moon in Capricorn
Moon enters Aquarius 2:21 pm

25 Saturday
Moon in Aquarius

26 Sunday
Moon in Aquarius
Moon enters Pisces 3:33 pm

27 Monday
Moon in Pisces

28 Tuesday
Moon in Pisces
Moon enters Aries 3:31 pm

29 Wednesday
Moon in Aries
New Moon 5:15 am

30 Thursday
Moon in Aries
Moon enters Taurus 4:00 pm

31 Friday
Moon in Taurus

1 Saturday
Moon in Taurus
Moon enters Gemini 6:49 pm

April Fools' Day

2 Sunday
Moon in Gemini

Daylight Saving Time begins at 2 am

3 Monday
Moon in Gemini

4 Tuesday
Moon in Gemini
Moon enters Cancer 2:15 am

5 Wednesday
Moon in Cancer
Second Quarter 8:01 am

6 Thursday
Moon in Cancer
Moon enters Leo 12:25 pm

7 Friday
Moon in Leo

8 Saturday
Moon in Leo

9 Sunday
Moon in Leo
Moon enters Virgo 12:58 am

Palm Sunday

10 Monday
Moon in Virgo

11 Tuesday
Moon in Virgo
Moon enters Libra 1:46 pm

12 Wednesday
Moon in Libra

13 Thursday
Moon in Libra
Full Moon 12:40 pm

Passover begins

14 Friday
Moon in Libra
Moon enters Scorpio 1:08 am

Good Friday

15 Saturday
Moon in Scorpio

16 Sunday

Moon in Scorpio
Moon enters Sagittarius 10:19 am

Easter

17 Monday

Moon in Sagittarius

18 Tuesday

Moon in Sagittarius
Moon enters Capricorn 5:13 pm

19 Wednesday

Moon in Capricorn

Passover ends

20 Thursday

Moon in Capricorn
Sun enters Taurus 1:26 am
Moon enters Aquarius 9:56 pm
Fourth Quarter 11:28 pm

21 Friday

Moon in Aquarius

Orthodox Good Friday

22 Saturday

Moon in Aquarius

Earth Day

23 Sunday
Moon in Aquarius
Moon enters Pisces 12:43 am

Orthodox Easter

24 Monday
Moon in Pisces

25 Tuesday
Moon in Pisces
Moon enters Aries 2:12 am

26 Wednesday
Moon in Aries

27 Thursday
Moon in Aries
Moon enters Taurus 3:27 am
New Moon 3:44 pm

28 Friday
Moon in Taurus

29 Saturday
Moon in Taurus
Moon enters Gemini 5:58 am

30 Sunday
Moon in Gemini

1 Monday
Moon in Gemini
Moon enters Cancer 11:17 am

Beltane

2 Tuesday
Moon in Cancer

3 Wednesday
Moon in Cancer
Moon enters Leo 8:18 pm

4 Thursday
Moon in Leo

5 Friday
Moon in Leo
Second Quarter 1:13 am

Cinco de Mayo

6 Saturday
Moon in Leo
Moon enters Virgo 8:20 am

7 Sunday
Moon in Virgo

8 Monday
Moon in Virgo
Moon enters Libra 9:10 pm

9 Tuesday
Moon in Libra

10 Wednesday
Moon in Libra

11 Thursday
Moon in Libra
Moon enters Scorpio 8:24 am

12 Friday
Moon in Scorpio

13 Saturday
Moon in Scorpio
Full Moon 2:51 am
Moon enters Sagittarius 4:56 pm

14 Sunday
Moon in Sagittarius

Mother's Day

15 Monday
Moon in Sagittarius
Moon enters Capricorn 10:59 pm

16 Tuesday
Moon in Capricorn

Census Day (Canada)

17 Wednesday
Moon in Capricorn

18 Thursday
Moon in Capricorn
Moon enters Aquarius 3:19 am

19 Friday
Moon in Aquarius

20 Saturday
Moon in Aquarius
Fourth Quarter 5:20 am
Moon enters Pisces 6:39 am

21 Sunday
Moon in Pisces
Sun enters Gemini 12:31 am

22 Monday
Moon in Pisces
Moon enters Aries 9:24 am

23 Tuesday
Moon in Aries

24 Wednesday
Moon in Aries
Moon enters Taurus 12:00 pm

25 Thursday
Moon in Taurus

26 Friday
Moon in Taurus
Moon enters Gemini 3:19 pm

27 Saturday
Moon in Gemini
New Moon 1:25 am

28 Sunday
Moon in Gemini
Moon enters Cancer 8:33 pm

29 Monday
Moon in Cancer

Memorial Day (observed)

30 Tuesday
Moon in Cancer

31 Wednesday
Moon in Cancer
Moon enters Leo 4:51 am

1 Thursday
Moon in Leo

2 Friday
Moon in Leo
Moon enters Virgo 4:17 pm

Shavuot

3 Saturday
Moon in Virgo
Second Quarter 7:06 pm

4 Sunday
Moon in Virgo

5 Monday
Moon in Virgo
Moon enters Libra 5:08 am

6 Tuesday
Moon in Libra

7 Wednesday
Moon in Libra
Moon enters Scorpio 4:41 pm

8 Thursday
Moon in Scorpio

9 Friday
Moon in Scorpio

10 Saturday
Moon in Scorpio
Moon enters Sagittarius 1:05 am

11 Sunday
Moon in Sagittarius
Full Moon 2:03 pm

12 Monday
Moon in Sagittarius
Moon enters Capricorn 6:19 am

13 Tuesday
Moon in Capricorn

14 Wednesday
Moon in Capricorn
Moon enters Aquarius 9:32 am

Flag Day

15 Thursday
Moon in Aquarius

16 Friday
Moon in Aquarius
Moon enters Pisces 12:05 pm

17 Saturday
Moon in Pisces

18 Sunday

Moon in Pisces
Fourth Quarter 10:08 am
Moon enters Aries 2:54 pm

Father's Day

19 Monday

Moon in Aries

20 Tuesday

Moon in Aries
Moon enters Taurus 6:23 pm

21 Wednesday

Moon in Taurus
Sun enters Cancer 8:26 am

Litha

22 Thursday

Moon in Taurus
Moon enters Gemini 10:49 pm

23 Friday

Moon in Gemini

24 Saturday

Moon in Gemini

25 Sunday

Moon in Gemini
Moon enters Cancer 4:48 am
New Moon 12:05 pm

26 Monday

Moon in Cancer

27 Tuesday

Moon in Cancer
Moon enters Leo 1:09 pm

28 Wednesday

Moon in Leo

29 Thursday

Moon in Leo

30 Friday

Moon in Leo
Moon enters Virgo 12:15 am

1 Saturday

Moon in Virgo

2 Sunday
Moon in Virgo
Moon enters Libra 1:06 pm

3 Monday
Moon in Libra
Second Quarter 12:37 pm

4 Tuesday
Moon in Libra

Independence Day

5 Wednesday
Moon in Libra
Moon enters Scorpio 1:13 am

6 Thursday
Moon in Scorpio

7 Friday
Moon in Scorpio
Moon enters Sagittarius 10:13 am

8 Saturday
Moon in Sagittarius

9 Sunday

Moon in Sagittarius
Moon enters Capricorn 3:25 pm

10 Monday

Moon in Capricorn
Full Moon 11:02 pm

11 Tuesday

Moon in Capricorn
Moon enters Aquarius 5:46 pm

12 Wednesday

Moon in Aquarius

13 Thursday

Moon in Aquarius
Moon enters Pisces 6:59 pm

14 Friday

Moon in Pisces

15 Saturday

Moon in Pisces
Moon enters Aries 8:39 pm

16 Sunday
Moon in Aries

17 Monday
Moon in Aries
Fourth Quarter 3:12 pm
Moon enters Taurus 11:44 pm

18 Tuesday
Moon in Taurus

19 Wednesday
Moon in Taurus

20 Thursday
Moon in Taurus
Moon enters Gemini 4:38 am

21 Friday
Moon in Gemini

22 Saturday
Moon in Gemini
Moon enters Cancer 11:28 am
Sun enters Leo 7:18 pm

23 Sunday
Moon in Cancer

24 Monday
Moon in Cancer
Moon enters Leo 8:24 pm

25 Tuesday
Moon in Leo
New Moon 12:31 am

26 Wednesday
Moon in Leo

27 Thursday
Moon in Leo
Moon enters Virgo 7:36 am

28 Friday
Moon in Virgo

29 Saturday
Moon in Virgo
Moon enters Libra 8:27 pm

30 Sunday
Moon in Libra

31 Monday
Moon in Libra

1 Tuesday
Moon in Libra
Moon enters Scorpio 9:08 am

Lammas

2 Wednesday
Moon in Scorpio
Second Quarter 4:46 am

3 Thursday
Moon in Scorpio
Moon enters Sagittarius 7:13 pm

4 Friday
Moon in Sagittarius

5 Saturday
Moon in Sagittarius

6 Sunday
Moon in Sagittarius
Moon enters Capricorn 1:19 am

7 Monday
Moon in Capricorn

8 Tuesday
Moon in Capricorn
Moon enters Aquarius 3:47 am

9 Wednesday
Moon in Aquarius
Full Moon 6:54 am

10 Thursday
Moon in Aquarius
Moon enters Pisces 4:10 am

11 Friday
Moon in Pisces

12 Saturday
Moon in Pisces
Moon enters Aries 4:22 am

13 Sunday
Moon in Aries

14 Monday
Moon in Aries
Moon enters Taurus 6:00 am

15 Tuesday
Moon in Taurus
Fourth Quarter 9:51 pm

16 Wednesday
Moon in Taurus
Moon enters Gemini 10:07 am

17 Thursday
Moon in Gemini

18 Friday
Moon in Gemini
Moon enters Cancer 5:03 pm

19 Saturday
Moon in Cancer

20 Sunday
Moon in Cancer

21 Monday
Moon in Cancer
Moon enters Leo 2:33 am

22 Tuesday
Moon in Leo

23 Wednesday
Moon in Leo
Sun enters Virgo 2:22 am
Moon enters Virgo 2:08 pm
New Moon 3:10 pm

24 Thursday
Moon in Virgo

25 Friday
Moon in Virgo

26 Saturday
Moon in Virgo
Moon enters Libra 3:01 am

27 Sunday
Moon in Libra

28 Monday
Moon in Libra
Moon enters Scorpio 3:56 pm

29 Tuesday
Moon in Scorpio

30 Wednesday
Moon in Scorpio

31 Thursday
Moon in Scorpio
Moon enters Sagittarius 3:00 am
Second Quarter 6:56 pm

1 Friday
Moon in Sagittarius

2 Saturday
Moon in Sagittarius
Moon enters Capricorn 10:34 am

3 Sunday
Moon in Capricorn

4 Monday
Moon in Capricorn
Moon enters Aquarius 2:15 pm

Labor Day

5 Tuesday
Moon in Aquarius

6 Wednesday
Moon in Aquarius
Moon enters Pisces 2:56 pm

7 Thursday
Moon in Pisces
Full Moon 2:42 pm

8 Friday
Moon in Pisces
Moon enters Aries 2:23 pm

9 Saturday
Moon in Aries

10 Sunday

Moon in Aries
Moon enters Taurus 2:30 pm

11 Monday

Moon in Taurus

12 Tuesday

Moon in Taurus
Moon enters Gemini 4:59 pm

13 Wednesday

Moon in Gemini

14 Thursday

Moon in Gemini
Fourth Quarter 7:15 am
Moon enters Cancer 10:53 pm

15 Friday

Moon in Cancer

16 Saturday

Moon in Cancer

17 Sunday
Moon in Cancer
Moon enters Leo 8:15 am

18 Monday
Moon in Leo

19 Tuesday
Moon in Leo
Moon enters Virgo 8:07 pm

20 Wednesday
Moon in Virgo

21 Thursday
Moon in Virgo

22 Friday
Moon in Virgo
New Moon 7:45 am
Moon enters Libra 9:06 am

23 Saturday
Moon in Libra
Sun enters Libra 12:03 am

Mabon ◆ Rosh Hashanah

24 Sunday
Moon in Libra
Moon enters Scorpio 9:54 pm

Ramadan begins

25 Monday
Moon in Scorpio

26 Tuesday
Moon in Scorpio

27 Wednesday
Moon in Scorpio
Moon enters Sagittarius 9:16 am

28 Thursday
Moon in Sagittarius

29 Friday
Moon in Sagittarius
Moon enters Capricorn 6:01 pm

30 Saturday
Moon in Capricorn
Second Quarter 7:04 am

1 Sunday
Moon in Capricorn
Moon enters Aquarius 11:24 pm

2 Monday
Moon in Aquarius

Yom Kippur

3 Tuesday
Moon in Aquarius

4 Wednesday
Moon in Aquarius
Moon enters Pisces 1:33 am

5 Thursday
Moon in Pisces

6 Friday
Moon in Pisces
Moon enters Aries 1:32 am
Full Moon 11:13 pm

7 Saturday
Moon in Aries

Sukkot begins

8 Sunday
Moon in Aries
Moon enters Taurus 1:04 am

9 Monday
Moon in Taurus

Columbus Day (observed)

10 Tuesday
Moon in Taurus
Moon enters Gemini 2:06 am

11 Wednesday
Moon in Gemini

12 Thursday
Moon in Gemini
Moon enters Cancer 6:21 am

13 Friday
Moon in Cancer
Fourth Quarter 8:25 pm

Sukkot ends

14 Saturday
Moon in Cancer
Moon enters Leo 2:38 pm

15 Sunday
Moon in Leo

16 Monday
Moon in Leo

17 Tuesday
Moon in Leo
Moon enters Virgo 2:15 am

18 Wednesday
Moon in Virgo

19 Thursday
Moon in Virgo
Moon enters Libra 3:19 pm

20 Friday
Moon in Libra

21 Saturday
Moon in Libra

22 Sunday

Moon in Libra
New Moon 1:14 am
Moon enters Scorpio 3:54 am

23 Monday

Moon in Scorpio
Sun enters Scorpio 9:26 am

24 Tuesday

Moon in Scorpio
Moon enters Sagittarius 2:53 pm

Ramadan ends

25 Wednesday

Moon in Sagittarius

26 Thursday

Moon in Sagittarius
Moon enters Capricorn 11:47 pm

27 Friday

Moon in Capricorn

28 Saturday

Moon in Capricorn

29 Sunday

Moon in Capricorn
Moon enters Aquarius 5:17 am
Second Quarter 4:25 pm

Daylight Saving Time ends at 2 am

30 Monday

Moon in Aquarius

31 Tuesday

Moon in Aquarius
Moon enters Pisces 9:10 am

Halloween/Samhain

1 Wednesday

Moon in Pisces

All Saints' Day

2 Thursday

Moon in Pisces
Moon enters Aries 10:46 am

3 Friday

Moon in Aries

4 Saturday

Moon in Aries
Moon enters Taurus 11:05 am

5 Sunday

Moon in Taurus
Full Moon 7:58 am

6 Monday

Moon in Taurus
Moon enters Gemini 11:46 am

7 Tuesday

Moon in Gemini

Election Day

8 Wednesday

Moon in Gemini
Moon enters Cancer 2:46 pm

9 Thursday

Moon in Cancer

10 Friday

Moon in Cancer
Moon enters Leo 9:34 pm

11 Saturday

Moon in Leo

Veterans Day

12 Sunday
Moon in Leo
Fourth Quarter 12:45 pm

13 Monday
Moon in Leo
Moon enters Virgo 8:18 am

14 Tuesday
Moon in Virgo

15 Wednesday
Moon in Virgo
Moon enters Libra 9:14 pm

16 Thursday
Moon in Libra

17 Friday
Moon in Libra

18 Saturday
Moon in Libra
Moon enters Scorpio 9:46 am

19 Sunday
Moon in Scorpio

20 Monday
Moon in Scorpio
New Moon 5:18 pm
Moon enters Sagittarius 8:15 pm

21 Tuesday
Moon in Sagittarius

22 Wednesday
Moon in Sagittarius
Sun enters Sagittarius 6:02 am

23 Thursday
Moon in Sagittarius
Moon enters Capricorn 4:25 am

Thanksgiving Day

24 Friday
Moon in Capricorn

25 Saturday
Moon in Capricorn
Moon enters Aquarius 10:41 am

26 Sunday

Moon in Aquarius

27 Monday

Moon in Aquarius
Moon enters Pisces 3:20 pm

28 Tuesday

Moon in Pisces
Second Quarter 1:29 am

29 Wednesday

Moon in Pisces
Moon enters Aries 6:30 pm

30 Thursday

Moon in Aries

1 Friday

Moon in Aries
Moon enters Taurus 8:26 pm

2 Saturday

Moon in Taurus

3 Sunday

Moon in Taurus
Moon enters Gemini 10:05 pm

4 Monday

Moon in Gemini
Full Moon 7:25 pm

5 Tuesday

Moon in Gemini

6 Wednesday

Moon in Gemini
Moon enters Cancer 1:00 am

7 Thursday

Moon in Cancer

8 Friday

Moon in Cancer
Moon enters Leo 6:52 am

9 Saturday

Moon in Leo

10 Sunday

Moon in Leo
Moon enters Virgo 4:31 pm

11 Monday

Moon in Virgo

12 Tuesday

Moon in Virgo
Fourth Quarter 9:32 am

13 Wednesday

Moon in Virgo
Moon enters Libra 5:00 am

14 Thursday

Moon in Libra

15 Friday

Moon in Libra
Moon enters Scorpio 5:42 pm

16 Saturday

Moon in Scorpio

Hanukkah begins

17 Sunday
Moon in Scorpio

18 Monday
Moon in Scorpio
Moon enters Sagittarius 4:10 am

19 Tuesday
Moon in Sagittarius

20 Wednesday
Moon in Sagittarius
New Moon 9:01 am
Moon enters Capricorn 11:39 am

21 Thursday
Moon in Capricorn
Sun enters Capricorn 7:22 pm

Yule

22 Friday
Moon in Capricorn
Moon enters Aquarius 4:49 pm

23 Saturday
Moon in Aquarius

Hanukkah ends

24 Sunday

Moon in Aquarius
Moon enters Pisces 8:43 pm

Christmas Eve

25 Monday

Moon in Pisces

Christmas Day

26 Tuesday

Moon in Pisces

Kwanzaa begins

27 Wednesday

Moon in Pisces
Moon enters Aries 12:04 am
Second Quarter 9:48 am

28 Thursday

Moon in Aries

29 Friday

Moon in Aries
Moon enters Taurus 3:08 am

30 Saturday

Moon in Taurus

31 Sunday
Moon in Taurus
Moon enters Gemini 6:16 am

New Year's Eve

1 Monday
Moon in Gemini

New Year's Day ✦ Kwanzaa ends

2 Tuesday
Moon in Gemini
Moon enters Cancer 10:14 am

3 Wednesday
Moon in Cancer
Full Moon 8:57 am

4 Thursday
Moon in Cancer
Moon enters Leo 4:14 pm

5 Friday
Moon in Leo

6 Saturday
Moon in Leo

The Year 2007

January

S	M	T	W	T	F	S
	1	2	3	4	5	6
7	8	9	10	11	12	13
14	15	16	17	18	19	20
21	22	23	24	25	26	27
28	29	30	31			

February

S	M	T	W	T	F	S
				1	2	3
4	5	6	7	8	9	10
11	12	13	14	15	16	17
18	19	20	21	22	23	24
25	26	27	28			

March

S	M	T	W	T	F	S
				1	2	3
4	5	6	7	8	9	10
11	12	13	14	15	16	17
18	19	20	21	22	23	24
25	26	27	28	29	30	31

April

S	M	T	W	T	F	S
1	2	3	4	5	6	7
8	9	10	11	12	13	14
15	16	17	18	19	20	21
22	23	24	25	26	27	28
29	30					

May

S	M	T	W	T	F	S
		1	2	3	4	5
6	7	8	9	10	11	12
13	14	15	16	17	18	19
20	21	22	23	24	25	26
27	28	29	30	31		

June

S	M	T	W	T	F	S
					1	2
3	4	5	6	7	8	9
10	11	12	13	14	15	16
17	18	19	20	21	22	23
24	25	26	27	28	29	30

July

S	M	T	W	T	F	S
1	2	3	4	5	6	7
8	9	10	11	12	13	14
15	16	17	18	19	20	21
22	23	24	25	26	27	28
29	30	31				

August

S	M	T	W	T	F	S
			1	2	3	4
5	6	7	8	9	10	11
12	13	14	15	16	17	18
19	20	21	22	23	24	25
26	27	28	29	30	31	

September

S	M	T	W	T	F	S
						1
2	3	4	5	6	7	8
9	10	11	12	13	14	15
16	17	18	19	20	21	22
23	24	25	26	27	28	29
30						

October

S	M	T	W	T	F	S
	1	2	3	4	5	6
7	8	9	10	11	12	13
14	15	16	17	18	19	20
21	22	23	24	25	26	27
28	29	30	31			

November

S	M	T	W	T	F	S
				1	2	3
4	5	6	7	8	9	10
11	12	13	14	15	16	17
18	19	20	21	22	23	24
25	26	27	28	29	30	

December

S	M	T	W	T	F	S
						1
2	3	4	5	6	7	8
9	10	11	12	13	14	15
16	17	18	19	20	21	22
23	24	25	26	27	28	29
30	31					

The Hermit

For Further Study

L'EREMITA
L'ERMITE
IX
THE HERMIT
EL ERMITAÑO

DER EREMIT
DE KLUIZENAAR

The *RWS* Minor Arcana

by Mary K. Greer

The most influential tarot deck of the twentieth century is undoubtedly the *Rider-Waite* deck (published in 1909), here called the *Rider-Waite-Smith* deck in order to acknowledge its conceptualizer, Arthur Edward Waite, and its artist, Pamela Colman Smith. One of the chief mysteries regarding its creation is who devised the innovative storytelling images on the Minor Arcana and why. Waite gave us one reason: the pictorial devices are a "great help to intuition."

He explained in *The Pictorial Key to the Tarot*, "The mere numerical powers and bare words of the meanings are insufficient by themselves; but the pictures are like doors which open into unexpected chambers, or like a turn in the open road with a wide prospect beyond." Tarot readers are clearly meant to use the pictures as "hints of possible developments" since "the field of divinatory possibilities is inexhaustible." Furthermore, when applying intuition to the images, "the specific meanings recorded by past cartomancists will be disregarded in favour of the personal appreciation of card values." Waite expected readers to find their own meanings in the cards. But what has never before been revealed is that he also imparted a hidden dimension to the Minor Arcana by having them illustrate the great mystical quest literature.

First, let's review how the deck came about.

Waite told us a little about the "how" in his autobiography, *Shadows of Life and Thought*:

> It seemed to some of us in the circle that there was a draughtswoman among us who, under proper guidance, could produce a Tarot with an appeal in the world of art and a suggestion of significance behind the Symbols which would put on them another construction than had ever been dreamed by those who, through many generations, had produced and used them for mere divinatory purposes. My province was to see that the designs—especially those of the important Trumps Major—kept hidden . . . that which belonged to certain Greater Mysteries, in the Paths of which I was travelling.

It was not just the Trumps that contained the Greater Mysteries, for Waite's Minor Arcana deliberately depicted certain works that have carried these mysteries into modern times. While Waite was careful not to reveal the oath-bound attributes of the Hermetic Order of the Golden Dawn (a fellowship of ceremonial magicians founded in 1888), he made sure his readers knew that something called the "Secret Tradition" was veiled by the tarot symbols. This was a "doctrine of mystical death and rebirth found only in mystical experience, not in belief [i.e., religion] or philosophy." The western mystery schools from Eleusis through the Grail myths and into Freemasonry preserved its symbols and teachings.

Waite hated to admit that he owed any debt of knowledge to the Golden Dawn, and he only grudgingly did so: "I am not of course intimating that the Golden Dawn had at that time any deep understanding by inheritance of Tarot Cards; but, if I may so say, it was getting to know under my auspices that their Symbols—or some at least among them—were gates which opened on realms of vision beyond occult dreams." In fact, he banked on the importance of images in carrying the deepest of meanings.

Several factors suggest that the artist, Pixie Smith (as she was known to her friends), was much more involved in the design of the Minors than in that of the Majors. Waite explained that she already had "some knowledge of Tarot values," for Smith was also a member of the Golden Dawn. Perhaps Waite simply gave Smith a list of meanings and she formulated scenes that would illustrate them. Many of the motifs exist in her other artwork (see *The Encyclopedia of the Tarot, Vol. III* by Stuart Kaplan and "Holly's *Rider-Waite* Site" http://home.comcast.net/~vilex/). Furthermore, the images on several of the cards depart from Waite's descriptions, as though he were not truly familiar with them (consider the Six, Seven, and Page of Swords, and the Eight and Ten of Pentacles, among others). Waite also acknowledged that they had "other help from one who is deeply versed in the subject." This person is generally believed to have been W. B. Yeats, Florence Farr, or Arthur Machen (Waite's closest friend and collaborator in his Grail studies), all members of the Golden Dawn.

Waite had read all the major tarot commentaries, several of which he translated from the French, and he put the interpretations together to construct what he saw as a "harmony of the meanings which have been attached to the various cards." Among these were interpretations written by Etteilla in the eighteenth century and traditional playing card meanings such as those recorded by Robert Chambers in his 1864 *Book of Days*. Numerous antique decks were available at the British Museum, including the fifteenth century Sola Busca cards, which featured some Minor Arcana illustrations appropriated by Waite and Smith.

Known for his works on alchemy, ceremonial magic, devil worship, tarot, the Grail, Freemasonry, the Rosicrucians, Kabbalah, and Christian mysticism, Waite saw all these as secret schools of

sacred teachings that concealed the deeper mystery involving the individual's potential relationship to divinity, which he called the Secret Tradition.

The Secret Tradition consists of symbolic lore showing how a person is to make his or her heart into a sacred sanctuary and there undergo "an intimate union which constitutes what is called mystically the marriage of the Hierophant." The Hierophant's spouse is "the Shekinah [feminine face of God] restored to the Sanctuary." Thus, the Secret Tradition shows the way to the immanent presence of God and the realization of that presence. Waite felt the most important thing was an entering into the "deeper understanding" veiled by the external forms of the stories and symbols. As he wrote in *The Holy Grail*, "Everything depends on the individual mind's capacity to make unto itself a living meaning behind the Symbols and the Sacraments." This requires going beyond faith to a direct experience of divine will via what he termed "internal organs of higher consciousness."

Waite was convinced that "on the highest plane the Tarot offers a key to the Mysteries"; however, the Golden Dawn documents were "replete with Tarot symbolism of the inferior, magical kind." For Waite, it was the Grail myths that would add the deepest hidden meanings and a perennial quality to the *Rider-Waite-Smith* Minor Arcana. Despite his unequivocal hints, these have never before been specifically identified. Waite recognized that the higher significance of the Minor cards resides primarily within these mysteries.

In *The Hidden Church of the Holy Graal*, which was published the same year as the tarot deck, Waite pointed out that the sacred objects or symbols of Celtic lore mirror the four symbols sacred to Christ's Passion and central to the Grail legend. He declared that the "Hallows, under a slight modification, . . . are in the antecedents of our playing cards—that is to say, in the old Talismans of the Tarot."

The four Hallows of the Holy Grail and Celtic Mysteries are:

1) The Grail itself as Cup or Chalice, the Cup of the first Eucharist and the Cauldron of Plenty belonging to Dagda in Celtic myth.

2) The Spear of Longinus or of the Celtic God Lugh (Wands), which Waite said is also "the wounding for our iniquities, by which the life flowed from the body, and the issue of blood therefrom is the outgoing of the divine life for our salvation."

3) The Paschal Dish or Paten (Pentacles), which in Celtic myth is the Lia Fail, the Stone of Destiny, which indicated the rightful king.

4) The Sword symbolizing the Body of Christ; "its fracture is the bruising for our sins and the breaking for our trespasses, while at some far distance the resoldering signifies the Resurrection." It is also the Sword of Nuadu.

ACE ♣ CUPS.

"The four Hallows are therefore the Cup, the Lance, the Sword and the Dish, Paten or Patella—these four, and the greatest of these is the Cup," concluded Waite.

It was in the Grail stories that Waite found themes that became central to the suit cards. "These quests are mirrors of spiritual chivalry, mirrors of perfection, pageants of the mystic life, . . . and they offer in romance form a presentation of the soul's chronicle." In case we are in danger of missing this, Waite makes his intention very clear when he says the Ace of Cups is "an intimation of that which may lie behind the Lesser Arcana."

The Suit of Cups

In *The Hidden Church of the Holy Graal*, Waite retells the earliest of the Grail stories—Robert De Borron's *Metrical Romance of Joseph of Arimathea*, in which Joseph carries the Graal Vessel and "knowledge of the Secret Words" out of Israel. In the following summary, taken from Waite's telling, we can easily see the suit of Cups:

Ace of Cups On Good Friday, by the descent of a dove from heaven, carrying a sacred Host . . . the "crown of all earthly riches" was renewed. There is the flight of the mystical dove from the casement to inmost Shrine, as if the bird went to renew the virtues of the Holy Graal. The cup is now the receptacle of the graces which are above and the channel of their communication to things which are below.

2 of Cups	Joseph of Arimathea received the Grail (symbolizing Christ's love for humanity) into his keeping.
3 of Cups	On his journey, Joseph is accompanied by companions. At first they were in a state of grace.
4 of Cups	They departed from that grace through the sin of luxury.
5 of Cups	The result was a famine in the company.
6 of Cups	Brons took counsel with Joseph.
7 of Cups	Joseph invoked the Son of God on his knees in the presence of the Grail and Christ appeared to him. (In Perceval, there is a series of transformations of the Grail at the altar, culminating in some "undeclared Mystery.")
8 of Cups	Christ ordained that Brons should repair to a certain water and there angle for a fish.
9 of Cups	The Sacred Vessel was to be exposed openly in the presence of the brethren on a table similar to that of the Last Supper and the fish placed there. Whoever was seated thereat had the accomplishment of his heart's desire.
10 of Cups	Great delight was experienced by the elect who were present and their hearts were penetrated by great joy.

The fish symbolism in the Cup court cards now takes on new meaning: "It was said that in the sight of the Graal true believers experience as much satisfaction as a fish, which, having been taken by a man in his hand [Page of Cups], escapes therefrom and again goes swimming in the sea." The fish is "the sign of spiritual sustenance, of Christ's presence among His faithful, and hence of the Eucharist." It also hangs around the neck of the King of Cups, so that we may assume he is the "Fisher King."

The Suit of Wands

The Wands suit is clearly the *Longer Prose Perceval* first told by Chrétien de Troyes, the second of the great Grail narrators, and completed by a variety of authors. The tale has "the touch of Nature [the sprouting wands] which takes us at once into its kinship."

Ace of Wands This is the lance or spear from which fiery blood flows. It is also reminiscent of the flowering staff that Joseph of Arimathea planted at Glastonbury to signify the resting place of the Grail.

2 of Wands Perceval arrives at a castle, views the Grail and Lance at a feast, but fails to ask what has caused the Lance to bleed and what the Grail signifies. He wakes alone.

3 of Wands He exits the castle, crosses the moat, and the drawbridge pulls up so he is cut off from the castle. He now must wander and learn, while the Fisher King awaits his return.

4 of Wands At Caerleon castle he is greeted by great feasting after which he vows to discover the answer to the Grail questions.

5 of Wands There follow "five years of hard adventure in Quest and Errantry" in which he "remembered nothing of God."

6 of Wands During this time he conquers sixty knights, then meets a company of Lords and Dames on barefoot pilgrimage.

7 of Wands They reproach him for warfaring on Good Friday, and tell him of a Hermit.

8 of Wands He searches for the Hermit who answers all his questions.

9 of Wands He repents his misdeeds and is purged. He climbs Mt. Dolorous where he is surrounded by crosses and must fasten his horse to a central pillar or go mad.

10 of Wands He finally returns to the Grail castle, fulfills a task, but fails to heal the King. In some versions he now becomes the Guardian, with all its burdens and responsibilities.

The Suit of Pentacles

Waite recounts no specific myth in the Grail cycle that centers on

the dish or paten, so here we pick up the theme of Freemasonry, the foundation stone for rebuilding the Temple in the modern world. The story of the erection of an external building veiled a divine mystery. In *The Encyclopedia of Freemasonry* and *The Secret Tradition in Freemasonry*, Waite describes how "the degrees of Craft Masonry have as a main object the building up of the Candidate into a House or Temple of Life." When the Master Builder of the Temple of Jerusalem perished, the plans for an externalization of doctrine in the world was lost. It has been replaced by a path of symbolism.

Ace of Pentacles The Candidate is like a fruitful ground fitted to receive a seed. He has entered a path of experience, heretofore untraveled.

2 of Pentacles The institution must decide whom it will receive and whom deny. The candidate enters a realm of "double meaning" which is designed to show that there is a mystery of wisdom and sanctity, which is represented as lost by a revolt in the camp of initiation itself.

3 of Pentacles When the lodge opens for a candidate he enters an institution, symbolic of that state he is called to attain, for he is to be erected into a perfect building. A mallet and a chisel with a round head are presented to him. Master Architects are called to testify whether one of them is in possession of a design. Three rule a lodge, because man is constituted of body, spirit, and soul.

4 of Pentacles	The candidate is told he is the cornerstone of a new foundation from which he must build up himself. The original foundation was built on the prophets, then the apostles, and now on "living stones."
5 of Pentacles	This shows the loss of the Word and the period of decay, the poverty of spirit and denuded condition of those who have not as yet been enriched by the secret knowledge of the Holy and Royal Art.
6 of Pentacles	Those who receive the candidate stand in a superior place. They can confer what he does not possess—gifts of the magical formula—the want of which he is conscious. That in which they differ is also that which they can dispense to him.
7 of Pentacles	The initiate is restored to light; but it is to find himself encompassed by signs and symbols whose true value he may not yet perceive. These are the first fruits of Redemption in spiritual resurrection. He must show restraint and self-denial.
8 of Pentacles	Extending before him is a symbolic mode of ascent—Jacob's Ladder—the line of transcension by which the kingdom of earth is taken up into a kingdom not of this world. He passes through the grades and opening of the "seals" of the Old Covenant. He will find also the secret stars of the microcosm and the macrocosm.
9 of Pentacles	As Raised Master Mason, he has come to the place of the indwelling glory—the Shekinah in her Sanctuary. The grapes are a symbol of life and blood.
10 of Pentacles	This suggests the Royal Arch Grade, which puts forth the mystery of Christ as what was always concealed in the tradition of Israel. The Sacred House of Masonry is a House of Israel and a House Spiritual. The

temple is built within. The candidate springs
up and flourishes as a Tree of Life.

The Suit of Swords

The suit of Swords, despite its specific references to the *Galahad Quest*, seems to have a unique focus with at least three referents. Essentially, it represents the loss of the true mystery of Divine Immanence, and the sorrows we feel as the result of this loss, wherever this loss occurs. The core referents are:

1) The failure of Galahad to bring the Grail back into the world. This includes the perennial injury of the Fisher King and "the fatality [10 of Swords] that follows failure [7 of Swords] to ask the question, 'Whom does the Grail serve?'"

2) The unbelievers in Joseph of Arimathea's band who sat unmoved at the Graal table and were therefore banished.

3) The failure, within Masonry, to ask the questions that would lead to an understanding of the deeper significance of the story of the Master Builder who is killed by his jealous brethren.

Ace of Swords	The Dolorous Sword, which "was made or broken under strange circumstances of allegory," and which wounded the Grail King. The crown identifies it as the sword of King David. It is the two-edged Intellect that both conquers and kills.
2 of Swords	Waite discusses two swords: 1) that of King David, and 2) one that smites the son of Joseph, which is to be soldered by he who accomplishes the Siege Perilous. We also see the soul in waiting.
3 of Swords	Either Perceval is given the sword and it flies into pieces, or the Grail King battles with it; it shatters and pierces him in the thigh. Those who sit unmoved at Joseph's Graal table are denounced "as guilty of the vile, dolorous sin." Waite likens them to those who practice Masonic rites without a deeper understanding and so fragment the higher purposes of the rite.

4 of Swords	The King (or order) lies ill. No recitation of the putative, all-powerful words can ever relieve his sickness.
5 of Swords	Those who were denounced at the Graal table "went forth out of the house of Joseph covered in shame." The sword's resoldering was a test of each questing knight, who all fail. In Masonry, it is the discord among the brethren.
6 of Swords	David's sword was "placed in a Mysterious Ship destined to sail the seas for centuries." This Ship of Solomon conveyed Galahad, Perceval, Bors, and the sword from point to point on their progress.
7 of Swords	Here is the failure to ask the question, which leads to the many adventures where some thing is always left undone. The teachings are left in plain sight but few know their true value. "The heroes of [intellectual] research offer no light. . . . They take the memory of a glorious vision but have not received communication of the last secrets."
8 of Swords	In Masonic initiation, the candidate "has not eyes to see in the light of the secret knowledge. He is hoodwinked without because he is blind within."
9 of Swords	In Masonry, the House of God (inner temple) is therefore—as long as it remains—in mourning.
10 of Swords	Here is the death of the Master Builder, as well as that of the many knights who perished on the quest. In the Welsh Perceval, it is the "Sword which broke and was rejoined and, in the stress of the last trial, was shattered beyond recovery."

Waite names the Knight of Swords Galahad, for Galahad was girded with the Sword of David, which he, like Arthur, had drawn from a stone. *The Quest of Galahad* "tells how the Warden of the Mysteries together with the Holy Things, was removed once and for all . . . [because] the world was not worthy."

Waite explains why it is necessary to follow initiation (Eight of Swords) with sorrow and death (Nine and Ten of Swords), "The Craft," he explains, "is a symbol of loss . . . vested in the weeds of widowhood." The Queen of Swords is a widowed woman and Freemasons used the term "the widow's son" as a sign of their order. Additionally, Masonry involves a mystery of death and resurrection, of which Waite said, "That death pictured in the Mysteries is therefore in no sense physical, but is mystical, like the resurrection which follows it."

The sacred literature of the Western Mystery Tradition substitutes in the external world for the "true mystery." In *The Hidden Church of the Holy Graal*, Waite wrote that the Secret Church (of which the Minor Arcana describe only the external form) is "like the still, small voice; it is heard only in the heart's silence, and there is no written word to show us how its rite is celebrated. . . . There are no admissions . . . the candidate inducts himself." The presence of the Hallows, in the Minors, "may preserve the king [that is, our Divine Essence] alive, but otherwise they cannot help him." It is to the Major Arcana that we must turn for further direction.

This article offers but a bare outline of the great themes Waite portrayed in the four tarot suits. Anyone who carefully reads his many works will find plenty of details with which to flesh out these sketches. This is but a beginning of a new appreciation of the hidden significance of the *Rider-Waite-Smith* tarot deck.

For Paul McGoldrick (a.k.a A. Grinder) in acknowledgement of his dedication to understanding the works of A.E. Waite and of his gracious assistance.

The Hermit

by Edain McCoy

The twenty-two cards that comprise the Major Arcana in any tarot deck are well-known archetypes representing the steps of the mythic Hero's Journey—a mythic structure as old as humanity and as familiar as a favorite movie.

The hero—or heroine, as the case may be—must start his quest as the Fool, the youth dancing blindly toward the precipice of a cliff, unaware of and unconcerned by any danger. We see the heart of the Fool in many young people who live life in a rush of passion without reason or thought, as though they are indestructible. Once our hero realizes he's the Fool, he begins to work his way through each step of the journey that corresponds to each of the successive Major Arcana tarot cards.

He next becomes the Magician, or at least he appears to be. He is depicted with all the tools and elements necessary to make magic or change his course in life. All options are open to him. We know this because the elongated, sideways 8 that symbolizes eternity spirals above his head. Still, questions remain: Will he use these gifts? Does he have any idea how he's supposed to use them? The card only speaks of the ability, not the deed. If he does know how to use them, can he be trusted to use them well? Does he have any idea that what he chooses to do today could affect his spirit for eternity?

We recognize several of the Hero's Journey cards as "resting" cards—ones that tell us it's time to step out of the rapids and do some serious introspection on dry land. One of the most obvious of these resting cards is the Hermit.

The Hermit is the ninth card in most tarot decks, a point just short of the halfway mark through the twenty-two–card journey. Our hero has worked through his need to put on a false façade to impress others (the Hierophant, number five), made difficult choices between energies pulling at him in different directions (the Lovers, number six), taken hold of the incompatible reins of the Chariot (number seven), and learned to make these opposing forces work together to move his spirit onward.

Taking and holding on to the reins of the Chariot is a major feat, requiring inner and outer discipline and the agility of young adulthood. Take a look at the Chariot in almost any deck and you'll find it being driven by a young person, not a hermit. This feat with the Chariot deems the hero worthy of moving forward in his journey, and it shows his Strength (number eight) of body and spirit.

The tools he was given as the fledgling Magician (number one) were used correctly. Our hero is capable . . . so far. Of that we do not doubt. So what does he do with his capabilities now? His future must be more than a show he puts on to impress others—or it ought to be. Where does he take these forces he's learned to control, and what do they mean for his future?

This is how he finds himself inside the card of the Hermit, one of the most taciturn archetypes in occultism.

In most tarot decks the card following the Hermit is the Wheel of Fortune (number ten). It represents the ever-turning ups and downs of our rollercoaster ride through life. From joy to sorrow, from triumph to tragedy, no life is complete without them all, and when the wheel spins it moves in relation to our energies, as well the energies of others who are pressuring the course of your life, whether they are conscious of doing so or not.

As the Hermit we may pause, take a deep breath, and meditate on the next best step because, after we spin our Wheel of Fortune, we receive our first taste of karma in the form of Justice (number eleven). Then we get another brief respite in the Hanged Man (number twelve), before we must dive back into the raging river of life where major transformations—both positive and negative— await us within the ultimate card of transformation, Death (number thirteen). There are some serious issues to understand and many lessons to absorb before leaving the peace and seclusion offered by the Hermit.

I never before associated the Hermit card with anything other than a caution to pause and look inward in a spiritual sense. I used it to reassess where I was in spirit, faith, and my place on the web of being. Until this year I had no idea that the card would ever speak to me of physical changes as well—changes linked to spiritual growth, but still very corporeal. Huh? Over the last twenty years the concept of the brain-body-mind connection has become almost mainstream. I wondered if I missed an important day in karma class.

As part of a wonderful group of Witchy women—most of us in the forty-five to fifty-five age range—I have been blessed to share in their transitions to Elderhood as many of them reached their Croning time, or chose to share their memories of that transition with the rest of us. We'll take all the information we can absorb. Those of us who have not made that transition know that it looms on our horizon. Just accepting that my body was changing as the Goddess intended, in profound ways, some welcome and some not, compelled me to turn inward to seek the peace and quiet necessary to think about this transition to Elderhood—a transition that comes to all of us, female and male—and the impact it should or should not have on my physical and psychological life.

Traditional Witchcraft has taught us that a Crone Witch is a woman who has reached menopause. All the sacred blood of life which once flowed from her now remains inside her. Her power of knowing has become her power of wisdom, and we look to her awesome strength of self to guide us when our night is darkest.

The Crone Witch's counterpart is the Sage Witch, a man of about the same age whose family is raised, freeing him to take his lifetime of knowledge and transform it into wisdom. Like the Crone, his many lifetimes of wisdom rest deep inside him, and we should honor him that he might share some of that stored wisdom with the rest of us.

IX The Seeker

The Seeker from *The Witches Tarot*

People often refer to these Elder Witches as being in the last third of life.

Huh?

Last third? No way.

I may not be youthful anymore, but I'm sure not ready to be a Crone with one foot in my grave and the other on a banana peel.

Whoa, horse! I leapt out of that racing Chariot and went off in search of the Hermit. I had some knowledgeable ammunition of my own to fire at the Old Man once I found him. As usual, he was standing on his isolated mountain top, his lantern held high, his face a mask of peaceful acceptance as he peered into the abyss below. I could choose to gaze into the abyss with him, and maybe learn something, or I could pick a fight.

9 THE HERMIT

LANCELOT IN EXILE

The Hermit from *Legend: The Arthurian Tarot*

I picked a fight. A bad choice, even though I believed my arguments were sound.

If Witches in their forties were in the last third of their lives, then life expectancy charts should show us all riding off with the Grim Reaper around age sixty. Oh no, something was way out of line with this. This was my body we were making generalizations about. I'd been living in it for a long time. Who knew it better than me? I was an individual of reason and science and, even though I was also a Witch, I knew all about actuarial tables and other statistics that help one calculate life expectancy. I'd once worked out the average age at which my grandparents and great-grandparents passed over, added in some actuarial data, and with cool logic I assessed my own life expectancy at 88.4 years. That would make 44.2 years my official entry point into middle age.

Last third of my life, my fanny! I shoved my paperwork and calculator into the face of the Hermit. To my surprise, he just stood there and let me rage like the self-absorbed charioteer I was until I was calm enough to reopen myself to his wisdom.

I knew, as did he, that I was already gripped with a need to turn inward rather than forming a Croning Coven as I'd planned. I enjoyed solitary Witchcraft, but I also have cherished memories of groups and covens who were like family to me. My putting off the formation of a Crone's Coven had nothing to do with my body-age.

I was a busy woman, stressed and rushed like everyone else, but that was all. I told the old Hermit I needed some time for just me. "I deserve time just for me," I argued. But that didn't mean I was also becoming a Crone at this same point in time. Did it?

The Hermit began speaking to me as one flesh-and-blood creature to another, not as one eternal soul to another. This was new. I was—I am—middle aged, with more than just another twenty years to live, I told him. The Hermit agreed. I was somewhere around the halfway point of my life just as he is somewhere around the halfway point in the journey through the Major Arcana.

All my righteous indignation deflated as if I'd been poked with a spear. Were the Hermit and I just arguing in favor of the same point?

As I studied the Hermit's obvious sense of soul peace, I knew he was telling me that I must make wise choices about my future now or I might not get another chance. I never expected that his words would be familiar. They echoed the fears my father expressed daily upon reaching his late forties. He knew he had to position himself in a larger, more prosperous place than the opportunities being offered to him represented. If not, he feared he would find himself a man in his midfifties with few choices, working hard for little gain. After three decades of life had passed by, I finally understood my father's frantic need to get himself into the right place as soon as possible.

As I came to that same fork in the road that he and all of us eventually reach, the remembered words of my father came pouring out of my own mouth. You know you're middle aged when you find, to your initial horror, that you're becoming one of your parents. The Hermit's message was one he'd given to each generation before me. The path I now chose would make turning back later almost impossible. I needed to do some serious thinking about where I was and where I wanted to be.

Many of us allow our inner selves to entwine around the heart of each Major Arcana card. We gaze at their symbols and, in time, we gain the wisdom to read them

IX THE HERMIT

The Hermit from *Medieval Enchantment: The Nigel Jackson Tarot* intuitively. We step inside them and their landscape becomes part of our inner lives, and their populace become either allies or enemies. This intuitive gift, this power of "knowing," is given by the Hermit, whose job it is to send us into the second half of our lives with more than just a renewed spirit, but also with a sense of purpose and a solid foundation of self-esteem, as we transition into the complex yet inevitable role of Elder Witch.

Tarot Stories

Literature and the Cards

by Diane Wilkes

W hat bond do *Wuthering Heights* and *One Flew Over the Cuckoo's Nest* share? If you want to find out, read on. . . . The above sentences illustrate a classic storyteller's technique—the teaser. It's a surefire way to keep a reader's interest . . . but I'm not sure it's an ethical one to use with querents who are seeking answers. On the other hand, there are many techniques in the storyteller's arsenal that can be helpful to a novice reader who wishes to learn to communicate more effectively with querents.

This article focuses on another aspect of connecting story to the tarot—a practice that has been in effect for some time now. There are a plethora of decks based on literature. Some are rooted in mythology: there are four or five devoted to the Arthurian legends alone, Greek mythology is explored in the *Mythic* and *Olympus* tarots, and the *Goddess Tarot* offers images derived from many cultures. Other literary decks include the *Dante*, based on the *Inferno*; the *Alice in Wonderland Tarot* based on the timeless novel by Lewis Carroll; the *Amber Tarot*, which is based on a series of fantasy novels by Roger Zelazny; and the *Blake Tarot*, which is based on William Blake's literary and artistic oeuvre. Several Shakespearean tarots are available, as well.

These decks vary greatly, both stylistically and in quality. I find decks that offer a story or myth rooted in the Golden Dawn interpretations for each card to be the most rewarding, because that's the tradition with which I—and many tarot readers who cut their teeth on the *Rider-Waite-Smith* or *Thoth* decks—am most comfortable.

Some find theme decks of any kind to be limiting. I think literature-based tarots have the potential to offer new layers of interpretation about the archetypal images, though it's important to remember that the story or story-section given for a specific card is just one facet of a card that contains multiple meanings. And if you collect and/or create stories for each of the cards, you will discover the one or ones that correspond to your individual style. By recognizing what you don't resonate with, you will get a sharper, clearer image of how you personally define the tarot archetypes. Use the stories you discover as a tool to expand your present understanding of the card, not as something to memorize and parrot when the related card comes up in a reading.

Over a decade ago, I decided to create my own tarot deck as a tool for understanding the tarot more fully. I sought a focus to tie things together, and explored numerous approaches (some of which were quite silly!) before settling on a "Storyteller Tarot"—a tarot with each card based on a specific story. A voracious reader, I had a wealth of stories from which to choose—and found that the selection process was the task that helped me understand the Major Arcana in a way I hadn't before.

Having said that, I am very aware that there is no one story that defines any of the cards (though some are definitely richer and more evocative than others!). What resonates for me may be something quite different for you, which is why I recommend this process for tarotists at any stage. Beginning readers will learn the card interpretations more quickly if they can associate a story with them, and more advanced enthusiasts will find that their understanding of the cards is enriched and deepened with each new story connection.

When I created the *Storyteller Tarot*, I decided not to limit myself to a narrow definition of the word "story." While some people believed the words "story" and "fiction" were interchangeable and synonymous, the fourth edition of the *American Heritage Dictionary of the English Language* defines story as "An account or recital of an event or a series of events, either true or fictitious." I felt comfortable basing cards on scenes and characters from novels, but also on films, songs, and even anecdotes about specific politicians.

I discovered fairly soon that what I thought was an innovative approach to the tarot—matching cards to literature—wasn't unique. Theodore Roszak's *Fool's Cycle/Full Cycle: Reflections on the Great Trumps of the Tarot* includes several classical literary tarot assignments, such as the Fool to Dostoevsky's *The Idiot* and the Lovers to Plato's *Symposium*. There was even another *Storyteller Tarot* deck in existence, but fortunately it did not have the same thematic approach as my deck, or I'd have felt completely lacking in originality.

Several years later, I was approached by a tarot publisher to create a deck and book. I wasn't sure if I should accept, but a friend of mine, a shaman who serves as my spiritual adviser, convinced me that I was meant to do it. She even suggested that there was someone in literature whose work I'd like to feature in a deck. I immediately thought of Jane Austen, whose books I had been reading and rereading since tenth grade, and quickly agreed to create a *Jane Austen Tarot* based on that conversation alone.

Nothing like an exhaustive, deliberative process to prepare for a successful project, I always say. I soon realized that I had set myself a major task: finding seventy-eight scenes within six novels that are remarkably similar in setting and structure. Austen doesn't write sweeping, action-packed novels—she described her art as a "little bit (two inches wide) of ivory" and I had to find seventy-eight

scenes and/or characters within that constrained landscape. That I was able to do so is a testament to Austen's gift for conveying human nature with all its complexities, creating characters and characteristics that are universal and, therefore, eternally relevant. As I reread each novel, hunting for tarot connections, each discovery increased exponentially my love for and familiarity with both the author and the tarot. My understanding of Jane Austen's oeuvre and the tarot became richer, more complex.

One of the most exciting things for me with the *Jane Austen Tarot* is the connections it allows me to make between cards. The Magician and the Chariot are brother and sister—Harry and Mary Crawford in *Mansfield Park*—and now I see the commonalities in these two cards in a way I didn't before. Both cards embody single-minded ambition, individuals who are "driven" to achieve their goals. Their methodology may be different, but they are literally blood relations.

Even when the characters aren't interconnected, we can learn a great deal from attributing stories to each card. Let's look at the Devil card through the lens of story and myth. In the Bible, Lucifer is the Devil, a beautiful angel fallen from grace. What makes him fall? The sin of pride. In the classic play *The Devil and Daniel Webster*, by Stephen Vincent Benet, we have a silver-tongued Devil, but Webster, a legendary orator, outsmarts him.

In the *Storyteller Tarot*, my Devil is based on a novel by Lisa Goldstein called *The Red Magician*, where a powerful rabbi works dark magic in order to maintain his rule over his Polish community. In his hubris, he ignores warnings that the Nazis are coming; his village is destroyed and he dies a broken, insane man. This interpretation reminds us that the Devil can take on unexpected guises.

Jane Austen's books contain cads—like Wickham and Willoughby—but no real Devils. The exception is *Lady Susan*, an early work that was published posthumously and is often not considered part of the Austen literary canon. Lady Susan Vernon has affairs with married men, manipulates and tortures her daughter and anyone else she perceives as weaker than she is, and is a masterful, highly effective liar. Lady Susan is completely conscienceless, another silver-tongued Devil who employs her multifarious machinations in order to maintain power over everyone with whom she comes in contact.

You can see how each version of the Devil is rooted in traditional interpretive grounds, yet sprouts uniquely colored seeds with which to adorn and grow your reading garden. I am sure you can think of a time when you had dealings with a silver-tongued devil—or were in a relationship where someone was imposing his or her will on you and you felt chained and helpless, unable to escape. What is that story? What details bring it to life? Would this be a good anecdote to add to your collection of mental tarot meanings for the Devil card? Or the Eight of Swords, perhaps? The subtle details of your story will help you decide which card best fits the situation.

Personal anecdotes aren't the only stories you can connect with the cards. Scenes and characters from your favorite books and movies might illustrate the archetypes for you as well. You can make these connections by thinking of a specific card and trying to match it to a story, or, conversely, think of movies, books, or even personal episodes that have made their way into your family mythology that reflect a particular card.

Perhaps there is a political figure you admire—or detest. What anecdotes about them illustrate an archetype for you? When I chose Harry S. Truman for the Emperor for the *Storyteller Tarot*, all I knew about him was his famous expression, "The buck stops here." This phrase really spoke to me of the upright Emperor, one who would own responsibility for his actions. After reading several books about Truman, I was delighted with my choice. I discovered many anecdotes that expressed other facets of the Emperor. My favorite was the story that expressed the Protective Father archetype: when Truman's daughter performed a concert that received a negative review, the president wrote the critic a nasty letter, threatening to punch him if he met him on the street! And my reversed Emperor in the *Storyteller Tarot* was based on Frank Rizzo, a man without a high school diploma who worked his way up through the Philadelphia Police Department to achieve the position of Chief—and then became Mayor. He rose and ruled through brute force, not reason, and power was for him an end as well as the means. His high school yearbook ascribed a motto to him quite different from Truman's: "I didn't do it." The anecdotes involving these two very dissimilar men illustrate the upright and reversed aspects of the Emperor in memorable and distinct ways. Sometimes truth is not only stranger than fiction, but, when couched in the terms of story, can tell a memorable tale.

Recently, I got involved in a mail art project. The assignment: create a tarot card based on literature, ideally a relatively well-known novel. My first instinct was to choose one of my favorite classics, *Wuthering Heights*, and I decided that the separate demons that kept Heathcliff and Cathy enslaved and apart (his obsession, her need for societal status) would make a fine concept for the Devil card. I wasn't sure how I was going to illustrate it, but I envisioned blacks and reds, a palette of dark passion.

A few days later, my mouth dropped open as my husband and I were watching the movie *One Flew Over the Cuckoo's Nest*. The scene of the all-powerful Nurse Ratched, standing behind her antiseptic and safe glass window as she administers medication to a line of broken, hopeless men who know—and accept—that they will be force-fed their pills if they refuse to take them, is a horrifying and powerful depiction of the Devil. To me, Nurse Ratched's plasticene face beaming a seemingly benevolent smile as she numbs and cripples helpless men is far more terrifying than any horned beast.

Both these versions of the Devil are valid, yet a reader would rightfully interpret them differently, depending on the image used. The best readers have a number of possible interpretations for each card, and are able to select the most appropriate legend to tell the querent's story. The key is not to find *the* perfect tale for each card. but to connect various stories that broaden and expand the meaning of the cards; the more, the better. Not every one will work for every occasion, but, depending on the images and surrounding cards, each story can add another layer of possibility, another nuance, another potential meaning. The only danger is in dogmatically believing each card has but one story. That's when you become chained and limited, like the hapless prisoners in the Devil card.

Tarot & Ritual

The Aces

by Bonnie Cehovet

We all perform many ritual acts in our lives—whether we realize it or not. One of my favorite rituals is sitting on the porch with my first morning cup of coffee, watching the new day dawn and listening to the calls of the birds and other animals. Holidays are also a time of ritual for me. Baking, cooking, setting out decorations, getting together with family and friends—this marks life for me, and brings me joy. I do personal rituals on Full and/or New Moons, sometimes a small act, sometimes very formalized, depending on what is needed. This helps me anchor my life.

In the tarot world, we also perform many rituals, including some that we may not even consciously be aware of. Shuffling a deck to clear the energy is a form of ritual. Ordering the deck to clear the energy before we put it away is a form of ritual. Meditating on the cards is a slightly more formal form of ritual. Asking that our higher self (and the higher self of the seeker, if we are reading for someone else) guide the reading is a form of ritual.

One of the ways that we can consciously use ritual in relation to the tarot is to work with the archetype of a specific card—through meditation, entering the card, or including the card in formal ceremony. For the most part, work like this is done with the Major

Arcana. But there is another set of cards that offer a whole new world of exploration, and these are the Aces.

We normally think of the Aces as embodying the full elemental potential of their respective suits, and we like to see them come up in a reading because they represent new beginnings and fresh energy coming into our lives. But they are much more than this. They also reflect the four worlds (*Asiyah*, *Briyah*, *Yetzirah*, and *Atziluth*), the four seasons, and the four directions. A ritual journey with one or more of the tarot Aces serves to connect us with where we came from, where we are, and where we're going. It can help clarify and define our path, and help us remember our full potential in this lifetime.

The first thing that we need to do is to take a look at the world of the Aces, and what each one represents.

Ace of Wands
Element: Fire
Quality: Energy
Direction: South
Season: Spring
World: Asiyah (Yod)

Ace of Cups
Element: Water
Quality: Feeling
Direction: West
Season: Summer
World: Briyah (Heh)

Ace of Swords
Element: Air
Quality: Thought
Direction: East
Season: Fall
World: Yetzirah (Vav)

Ace of Pentacles
Element: Earth
Quality: Matter
Direction: North
Season: Winter
World: Atziluth (Heh)

Now we have the background for our ritual journey. We can journey with one Ace at a time, or with all four of the Aces together. The path we choose will depend to a large extent on why we are taking the journey. If we want to address a specific area of our life, we will choose to journey with the card that represents that energy. For example, if my concerns were centered around creativity in my life, I would journey with the Ace of Wands. If they were about some aspect of a relationship, I would journey with the Ace of Cups. If my concern was about mental/intellectual issues—looking for the truth about something—then I would journey with the Ace of Swords. If my concern was about issues of security or anything to do with the physical/material world, then I would journey with the Ace of Pentacles.

Journeying is all about using our imagination to visit different realities. It takes us beyond our self-imposed boundaries and shows us what lies beyond those edges. Accessing our imaginations allows us to better understand ourselves, and to grow personally and spiritually. In *Magical Pathworking* (Llewellyn 2004), author Nick Farrell takes this one step further in discussing what he calls "magical imagination." The use of magical imagination allows us not only to visit our imagination, but also to change our consciousness—how we choose to see things—which then allows us to transform ourselves and our environment.

Let's take a magical ritual journey with one of the Aces (a journey with all four Aces is possible, but would be much more complex; I want to present a ritual journey here that is easy to take, one that will act as a catalyst, perhaps, for further travels). The following steps are how I would build my journey. Take from this whatever resonates with you, and make it part of your journey.

1. Decide why you are taking the journey, e.g., What is your intent? Are you addressing a personal life issue? Are you celebrating a new season coming in? Are you exploring one of the Kabbalistic worlds? Are you attempting to understand the tarot Aces better? Keep your intention in mind.

ACE OF SHIELDS

EVALACH'S SHIELD

The Ace of Shields from *Legend: The Arthurian Tarot*

2. Make sure that the environment for your journey is conducive to exploration and learning. The physical area should be one that is quiet, and where you will not be disturbed. You may wish to play soft background music, set out some beautiful flowers (or a potted plant), or burn some incense. You have the power to create a safe, nurturing environment for yourself.

3. Before you begin your journey, do a short relaxation exercise so that you are not carrying the day's worries with you. Sit (or lie down) in a comfortable position. Close your eyes and take a deep breath. As you exhale, feel your cares being lifted from your shoulders. Feel yourself becoming lighter and lighter. Continue focusing on your breathing until you feel completely cleared.

4. If you wish to work with specific entities, guides, or your higher self, or if you wish to ask a totem animal to accompany you, now is the time to do that. Simply ask them to join you, either out loud or in your mind.

5. Ground yourself. Grounding provides us with a balanced state for our work. It centers us and allows us to concentrate. The following is only one example of a grounding exercise; use whatever works for you.

6. Seat yourself in a comfortable position. Take a series of three deep breaths, forcefully expelling them. As you breathe in the fourth breath, see yourself surrounded by the color red. Breathe in the color red and feel it expand to all parts of your body. As you exhale, feel the energy moving through the soles of your feet and into the earth. Take another breath, and see yourself surrounded by the color orange. Breathe in the color orange and feel it expand to all parts of your body. As you exhale, feel the energy moving through the soles of your feet and into the earth. Repeat this sequence through all the remaining colors: yellow, green, blue, and purple. Lastly, breathe in the color white and feel it expand to all parts of your body. As you exhale, feel the energy moving through the soles of your feet and into the earth. Take a moment to feel the peace and serenity around you.

7. Set your intention. State the purpose of your journey.

8. Take up the tarot Ace that you have chosen to work with. Gaze at the card and allow the edges to soften and go out of focus. Feel yourself moving forward into the card and becoming part of it. How do you feel? Do you feel hot or cold? What are your emotions? Joyful? Sad? Anxious? Take a moment to relate to the atmosphere around you. You are in a space of pure energy—energy that has not manifested, so there will be no people in the card to talk to. The emotions that you feel, the experiences that you have, are how you relate to the energy that the card represents. Greet the energy, and ask if it wants anything from you. If it asks a question, politely answer it. Ask the energy if you may ask questions. If it says no, thank it for its time and bring yourself back to reality. There will be another time for questions. If the energy is willing to answer questions, ask about whatever is important to you.

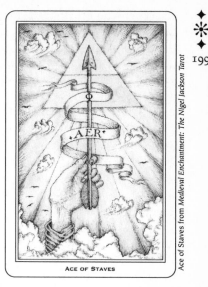

ACE OF STAVES

Ace of Staves from *Medieval Enchantment: The Nigel Jackson Tarot*

9. The following questions are examples of things that I might ask each of the four Aces. For the Ace of Wands: "What do I need to know about my creative nature? How can I best express my creative nature? Who am I in the world of Asiyah? What opportunities is this spring bringing to me?" For the Ace of Cups: "What do I need to know about my emotional nature? How can I best express my emotional nature? What do I need to know about the relationships in my life? Who am I in the world of Briyah? What new opportunities is this summer bringing to me?" For the Ace of Swords: "What do I need to know about my mental nature? How can I communicate better? How can I learn to make better decisions? Who am I in the world of Yetzirah? What new opportunities is this fall bringing to me?" And for the Ace of Pentacles: "What do I need to know about this side of my life? What do I need to do to create a safe place for myself? Where does my security come from? What seeds am I planting for my future? Who am I in the world of Atziluth? What new opportunities is winter bringing to me?"

10. When you are done asking your questions, thank the energy of the card and slowly bring yourself back into the real world. Take the time to tape or journal your thoughts about your journey and the new insights that were brought to you. Form an affirmation around the information that you were given so that the wisdom is planted firmly in your life.

The Aces are a world of opportunity for us. They are unexplored elemental energy waiting to be manifested, waiting to be put into use. What do you wish to manifest in your life? Which Ace, or combination of Aces, will assist you on your path?

Tarot Healing
Step by Step
by Corrine Kenner

You've probably heard of crystal healing sessions, in which healers lay crystals and stones on key power points of the body. Most healers focus on the *chakras*, the energy centers of the human body. Believers say that the energy of each crystal helps open blocked chakras, close overactive chakras, and ensure that all of the chakras work together in harmony.

While crystal healing can't replace conventional medical treatment and advice, it certainly can't hurt. In fact, crystal healing is a remarkably effective way to focus on good health in every aspect of life—body, mind, and spirit.

Crystal healing techniques can even be adapted to work with tarot cards. After all, crystals and tarot are complementary art forms; both embody the energy and vibrations that reflect the human experience.

If you are interested in experimenting with a tarot healing session based on crystal healing practices, here is a simple series of steps that you can try with a friend:

1. Dim the lights, light some incense or candles, and play soft background music.

2. Ask your friend to lie down on his or her back, either on a bed or on the floor.

3. Remind your friend to breathe deeply, in and out.

4. As your friend breathes, decide which cards you will lay on his or her major chakras. Start by choosing a card for the crown chakra, just above the head, and work your way down.

There are a number of ways to choose the cards. You can shuffle and lay cards at random, trusting the luck of the draw to select the correct card for each position. You can look through the deck, with the cards faceup, and use your intuition to find the right ones. You can even choose cards based solely on their visual appeal—just as crystal healers sometimes choose stones based on color and sensory appeal.

You can also consciously choose cards that work with the energy of each chakra. For example:

a) The crown chakra, just above the head, represents divine guidance. Try using The Star card.

b) The brow chakra, sometimes known as the third eye, represents perception and psychic ability. Try using the High Priestess card.

c) The throat chakra is connected to communication. Try using the Magician card.

d) The heart chakra relates to emotion, love, and compassion. Try using the Lovers card.

e) The solar plexus chakra is the seat of personal power. Try using the Emperor card.

f) The sacral chakra represents sexuality and creativity. Try using the Empress card.

g) The base chakra represents material existence. Try using the Fool card, or the World.

5. Also, choose a card for each hand, to reflect your friend's ability to give and receive. You might want to use the Ace of Wands or the Ace of Swords in the right hand, because both reflect active principals, and the Ace of Cups or the Ace of Pentacles in the left hand, to represent receptive ideals.

6. As you place the cards, visualize each chakra coming into perfect balance. Don't worry about trying to open or close the chakras, especially if you are not an experienced healer. Simply focus on balance, and let the universe do the rest. Also, as you lay each card, describe it and explain how it reflects the ideal energy of each chakra.

7. Work slowly. Once all the cards are in place, go back and remind your friend which cards are in which position.

8. Give your friend time to think about each of the cards, and discover whatever personal message they might hold. Take as long as you need: five minutes, or ten, or however long your friend wants to lie there.

9. Finally, remove each card. Once your friend sits up or stands, you can lay the cards out again on a table for review and further discussion.

As time goes by, you can adapt your tarot healing techniques to reflect the unique needs of your friends, family members, and clients. Ultimately, you might find that full-body healing spreads are almost more fun than tabletop readings.

A Closer Look At:

Medieval Enchantment

The Nigel Jackson Tarot

Created and illustrated by
Nigel Jackson

- 78 full-color cards, black organdy bag, and a 160-page minibook

- Cards are 4⅝ x 3¼, with nonreversible backs and illustrated pips

- Bold illustrations give ancient tarot styles a modern twist

- Cards are illustrated using the medieval symbolism from the first medieval tarot decks

- Minibook includes tarot history, spreads, and meditation techniques, and presents a new theory connecting the cards to Pythagorean numerology

The Three-Card "Drawing"

by Mary K. Greer

Many years ago, while I was teaching a five-day tarot workshop at the Omega Institute in Rhinebeck, NY, a man in the next cabin wanted me to look at his tarot journal. It was astonishing—on each page he had recorded a personal Celtic Cross spread entirely in drawings. The familiar layout could be discerned, but he had eliminated the borders on the cards, allowing the scenes to interpenetrate and the figures to interact. He said he got more out of intuitively playing with the pictures than from trying to interpret a reading in words. Indeed, his simple line drawings seemed so active, expressive, and alive. Here were pictures of his inner, psychic landscape—as deep and powerful as any dream. They were also reminiscent of medieval illustrations that depict a sequence of events in a single work.

When I complimented him on the quality of his drawings, he countered by saying that anyone could benefit by sketching the cards in their spreads. He suggested that I might want to start with a smaller spread, but that it wasn't the artistic skill that mattered.

Over the following years I kept seeing those enchanted drawings in my mind's eye, and hearing the recommendation of this chance-encountered, nameless, wise man. Yet I couldn't imagine doing it myself.

One day a student asked how she could learn to fully integrate the meanings of cards in her readings. It's not an unusual request— but suddenly I got it! I am always looking for experiential learning techniques that will bypass the intellectual mind and its gate-keeper, the critic, so I decided to have the class do three-card versions of the drawing. I wanted a medium that would disallow any fussiness or need for perfection and that would actually encourage playfulness, so I pulled out my giant box of 128 colored crayons. The experiment succeeded beyond my wildest dreams and has become one of my favorite teaching tools, plus a cherished method for generating my own insights. A few students have tried to dodge the process by producing something abstract, or even mad scribbles, but these have proven as effective as the more literal renditions, if not more so. I suggest starting simply, with stick figures and basic outlines. If you can play *Pictionary*, you can do the Three-Card Drawing.

This process demonstrates how to see the cards from a different point of view—no longer static or independent of each other, but dynamically interpenetrating, literally and figuratively. It's like switching to a different channel of perception from the ones through which we normally sense the cards. The doing of the drawing is so very different from thinking about it, and the latter can never substitute for the gestalt that occurs visually and as a physical awareness as you sketch. Let me be clear that I am not proposing to replace conventional tarot readings nor traditional interpretation, but to enhance skills and add possibilities.

In terms of personal insight, your knowledge and level of expertise in tarot has absolutely no bearing on your ability to do the process. Beginners and professionals can find it of equal value. If you teach, try it with your students.

You can do the process on your own, but doing it with one or two other people will intensify your focus and deepen insights through brainstorming and discussion.

The drawing generally works best on a standard sheet of white paper (turned either way), using crayons. (Watercolor crayons such as those by Caran d'Ache and Payons, or colored markers can be added for special effects.) Pens and pencils should be avoided until you've tried one or more drawings and are ready to modify the concept to reflect your own personal tastes and needs.

Working with different decks can produce surprising results. The *William Blake Tarot of the Creative Imagination* resulted, for me, in dreamy, energy-filled landscapes and softly smudged colors. *Nefer-tari's Tarot* became surrealistic, while I entered an emotional realm with the *Thoth* deck. By contrast, my *Rider-Waite-Smith*–based draw-ings were quite literal and prompted strong facial expressions.

Instructions

Materials needed:

- Standard white sheet of paper
- Crayons in lots of colors
- Three cards, selected facedown, from a tarot deck
- Twenty-minute time limit

Shuffle your deck while asking, "What do I most need to look at in my life right now?" This question can be modified by adding an area of interest or concern, such as, ". . . around relationships/money/my life path," or ". . . around my relationship with _____."

Cut the deck, restack, and draw three cards from the top, or fan the cards and select from anywhere. Turn your cards faceup and move them around, changing their order, stacking them in a pyra-mid, and even overlapping them. Watch for something to catch your eye. Imagine that the borders dissolve so that they all inhabit the same environment. Does a particular background take over? What person, form, or structure comes to the fore? Could you sub-stitute an element from one card to another?

Begin your drawing as soon as you get a hint of an image or theme—don't wait for the full picture. It will emerge in its own time and way. Let elements sur-prise you. You can use light-colored crayons to sketch in the stick figures, adding definitive lines, expressions, details, and clothing later.

Elements can be elimi-nated, relative sizes grow or shrink, images overlap. The "correct" number of suit markers (cups, wands, etc.) does not *have* to be maintained. Sometimes the images form a sequence of events; beware, however, of falling into the trap of separate meanings for each card, which this process seeks to transcend.

A timed session of twenty minutes will help you stay focused and moving along. You don't want to plan out your drawing before you begin or even think too much about what you're doing. Start with anything that strikes you. At the end of the twenty minutes use the side of a crayon to lightly shade sky, ground, or other large white areas, as this helps tie all the elements together. If you finish ahead of time, add details or intensify the colors.

Examples

Given the Page of Cups, Five of Cups, and Two of Pentacles of the *Rider-Waite-Smith* deck, this drawing showed the Page juggling a bunch of cups, several of which had fallen—including the cup with a fish, which now floundered on the river bank. In this case, one person took the place of three, blending all their actions.

In a drawing based on Death, the Six of Swords, and the Two of Pentacles, a skeleton poled a boat across a river with his scythe, while a person in the front of the boat juggled two pentacles; thus, the usual figures in the boat had been replaced. In the distance the Sun rose (or set) between a gate of swords.

In the case of the Moon, Four of Pentacles, and Hierophant, the Moon card provided its familiar landscape as background while Hierophant and the Midas-like figure, grasping his pentacles, substituted for the dog and wolf.

Perhaps a figure from one card moves toward or away from the figures on other cards. For instance, in another *RWS* drawing, the

cloaked person in the boat of the Six of Swords was depicted carrying a cup to the person in the Nine of Cups, who was sitting on a dock, while the person in the Two of Wands gazed down at them from his castle, holding another cup instead of a globe. With some modification, this drawing could have shown a sequence involving a person taking cups from his castle and transporting them by boat to the banquet.

In a *Thoth*-based drawing, a couple pledged their troth (Lovers) in the middle of a pea green swamp while, overlaid on the couple, seven cups dripped green slime (Seven of Cups). The overarching hermitlike figure behind the Lovers was crowned by giant red flames and lotuses (Three of Wands).

Working With Your Drawing

Now it's time to do what I call "working with your drawing." It's especially exciting to talk about it with other people, but you can explore and brainstorm on your own by writing your thoughts in a journal. The following questions are meant to stimulate thinking and suggest fruitful considerations. Feel free to use whatever works for you. Many dream techniques will be applicable. Keep the focus on the drawing itself, only occasionally contrasting it with the original cards.

1) Describe your picture.

- What's happening in it?
- How did you get from the cards to the drawing?
- Did anything surprise you?

2) Note the following and their possible significance:

- Choice of colors
- Energy flows (circular, jagged, grouped)
- Direction of movement
- Distance between objects
- Relative size (of people and things)
- Accidents

3) Find the main focus—where your eye is most strongly pulled. What does this suggest as the focus of your concern?

- What's at the center of your drawing?
- What and where are the major energy interplays?

4) Where or what are you in the picture? Speaking from this point of view:

- What are you doing?
- How do you feel?
- What do you want or need?
- Where do you want to go or what do you want to do next?

5) What or who are the other figures?

- What is the interaction between the "you" in item 4 and these figures?
- How are these other figures (and objects) also you?

6) Where are the greatest problems(s), obstacles(s), or stuck energy?

7) What is missing from the picture?

8) What is the task or opportunity in your picture?

- Is there something that needs to be changed for you to feel more empowered?

End your session by noting on the back of your drawing the following:

- Date (and optional brief notation of place and/or circumstances)
- Deck used
- Your three cards
- Title for the drawing
- One sentence summary—*in the first person, present tense,* describing what is going on in the picture. Do this, if nothing else!
- An action, task, or ritual suggested by the work that you now commit to doing within the next forty-eight hours.

Review your drawing and summary statement in three weeks, again in three months, and again in a year. Note any new insights concerning what your drawing presaged or brought into conscious awareness.

Where To Go From Here

Probably a few of you will dedicate a journal to sketches of your tarot readings. You'll adapt the process and materials to whatever suits your needs, and I hope you'll share your discoveries in the future. I'm not so consistent, but I have accumulated a dozen or so three-card drawings that I keep in a portfolio with plastic sheet protectors. It is surprising how each seems to mark a major turning point or realization in my life.

The next time you do a tarot reading (after having experienced the Three-Card Drawing) see if you can transfer what you've learned. Find the most important or confusing three cards in your spread and imagine their borders dissolving so that the scenes merge and the figures interact or blend or take on each other's characteristics. See if, by uniting seemingly disparate elements in an integrated vision, the central theme and key to the reading doesn't emerge. The spread position can lend nuances to your synthesis. For instance, a detail from a card in the "past," when blended with a detail from a "next step" card, will show how and where the past affects your next step. You have opened another channel of perception and learned to view your readings with new eyes.

A Closer Look At:
Animals Divine Tarot

Created and illustrated by Lisa Hunt
Foreword by Kris Waldherr

- 78 full-color cards, black organdy bag and a 216-page illustrated book

- Cards are 4⅝ x 3¼, with reversible backs and illustrated pips

- Major Arcana cards showcase sacred images and deities from myriad cultures, including Aztec, Incan, Indian, Roman, Egyptian, Greek, Japanese, African, and Native American

- Intricate watercolor paintings of animals on each pip card encourage the reader to reconnect with nature and tap into the world of animal energies

OTTER

TWO † CUPS

COYOTE

0 † THE FOOL

FOX

FIVE † PENTACLES

SPIDER WOMAN

XII † THE HANGED WOMAN

PANDA

TWO † PENTACLES

Justice
The Archetype of Balance
by Leeda Alleyn Pacotti

When we speak or think of an archetype, we are attempting to reach for an original pattern of idea or model of thought, which resides within every individual subconscious on the planet. Somehow, we know the prototype; we have an inkling. Yet, when we seek this archetypal reality in the physical world, we find it distorted by the perspectives of individual minds or patched together from a crazy quilt of misunderstood partialities. To find and understand the archetype of Justice, we must turn from the appearances of the everyday world, leaving behind the multitude of legal systems, which are too often colossal institutions of misjudgment, unevenness, and bias.

The Representation of Balance

In tarot decks following the Italianate sequence or that of the Hermetic Order of the Golden Dawn, Justice falls in the middle of the Major Arcana, coinciding with number eleven. This midpoint placement makes Justice a fulcrum, by which lower-numbered cards represent facets of individual consciousness or awareness, and cards of higher number suggest cosmic or universal consciousness.

As a demonstration of physical law, the fulcrum is a point without movement, which does not belong to or participate in the action of either side. At a moment of perfect balance, a seesaw suspended at the fulcrum makes a level plane, and the opposing sides have equal mass or weight. This is equilibrium, which cannot be disturbed by the opposing sides without some outside interference. With this example from the physical world, we have a better appreciation of the archetype of Justice, which can neutralize opposing elements without annihilating one or the other.

As mentioned before, many decks follow the Italian tradition, but some follow the French tradition instead, which drew heavily on the Italian. The major difference between these two systems is that the French sequence interchanges Justice with Strength, assigning Justice to number eight. From the glyph of the number eight (8), we still encounter a sense of balance, although it is vertical rather than the recognizable horizontal of eleven. It is possible that the French tarot decks suggest that balance is attained as an earlier state of conscious development, but it loses significance as the arbiter between the personal and the universal.

However, in nearly all tarot decks useful for occult study or meditation, the symbol of balance scales remains an intrinsic element of the design. Without regard for one placement over the other, within Justice reside balance and equilibrium.

Justice from *Medieval Enchantment: The Nigel Jackson Tarot*

VIII JUSTICE

Justice as Recompense

In early recorded history, society exacted justice by the standards detailed in the Old Testament of the Bible: "An eye for an eye; a tooth for a tooth." Remnants of this societal misunderstanding often crop up in our modern adjudicatory systems, in which we expect death for a murderer or castration for a rapist.

With more widespread education and an understanding that justice systems must teach as well as punish, modern societies have created penal systems, which impose a (hopefully appropriate) term of deprivation of freedom for those who transgress accepted laws, but also provide opportunities for them to delve into the motivations for their actions. Consequently, Justice is a woman, reflecting that the subconscious as well as the conscious is measured for recompense.

Here, Justice is the epitome of feminine objectivity or the quality of mercy, which stretches itself to judge those brought before it. Shall a swindler, whose victims include ruined families, be put to death or made to pay in time and fines? Shall a child of limited experience, knowledge, or maturity be treated as an adult? Shall the mother who gives up her children for their secure well-being be castigated with a lifetime of shame? Overtly, Justice attunes itself to the circumstance of the accused and to those wronged. Inwardly, it seeks the truth of motive, which may prove no wrong at all.

8 JUSTICE

Justice from *Ship of Fools Tarot*

Less obviously, Justice employs mental acuity and delineation of thought to discern the opposing pronouncements of each side. In its symbolism, Justice brandishes a sword with the blade rising, as a display of the higher mind of nobility that refuses to wallow in prejudicial slurs or bias. Her thoughts, like the honed edge of a rapier, slice through the morass of poor logic, specious sophistry, and exaggeration. Ultimately, her rendered verdict goes to the true nature of the wrongful thought or action. The punishment will fit the crime, but *only* the crime, without regard for silver-tongued oratory, emotional inveigling, or desperate wails of hardship from victims. Because the decisions of Justice are on target, we are assured that her pronouncements always provide improvement for those willing to look inward.

Justice as the Ultimate Law

In terms of human development, Justice has its finest moment as the true administrator of the ultimate law, karma. Justice is enthroned, elevated above the human condition and the jumble of erroneous thought. Woe unto those who believe they can escape punishment

Justice
Balance

Justice from *The Quest Tarot*

by hiding to the end of life, for the memory of Justice is eternal!

Once more we are brought to the archetype of balance, in which the ledgers of life are read and actions and thoughts are brought to account. What we do to harm ourselves and others are debits requiring adjustment. There will be no eye for an eye, no death for death. Instead, for failing to love, we will be given ample opportunity to love. For refusing consideration and mercy, we will receive experiences to broaden our perspective and change our minds. For disregarding lives, we will acquire responsibilities to nurture and support on both a small and large scale. In the end, we will be made compassionate, with certain knowledge of the right use of advantage and the pain of disadvantage.

Meditation on Justice

Usually, when we choose to focus on Justice, we approach it by thinking we will receive something back into our lives. Remember that Justice is impartial and does not stoop to pettiness. Far wiser we are to seek Justice as the threshold from individual awareness into cosmic consciousness.

When we wonder why we cannot move forward, Justice reveals misunderstandings and inconsistencies in our thoughts and actions. If we believe we deserve some restitution, Justice lets us know whether lack teaches us to understand the misuse of abundance. Should we investigate why we are so fortunate and gifted, Justice may well open the door to wider responsibility and the gentle secrets of the metaphysical realms.

Focusing on the major symbols in the Justice card helps evoke ways to attain a change in consciousness. Foremost, Justice is a woman, the intuitive repository of all laws governing the universe and the world; with mercy, she shows how we have mishandled or skirted these laws. To overcome the iniquities of daily life, we concentrate on her enthronement, which promises that noble, altruistic thoughts elevate us from the wretched mire. When we need clear, incisive thinking, we look to the rising blade of the sword, which cuts into both sides, leaving only the reliable kernels of truth. To regain our equilibrium inwardly or outwardly, we enter the image of the scales and their precise balance, where activity is at rest, and learn to make adjustments in ourselves.

Justice from *The Witches Tarot*

X Justice

Interpreting Justice for Divination

When using tarot cards for divination, Justice may take on either a positive or negative meaning, depending on our perspective (and without regard for her position as upright or reversed).

In understanding that Justice is impartial, unbiased, and objective, we must realize it does not champion a cause. Consequently, a positive or negative cast of meaning or interpretation projects from our own minds, in foolish attempts to link a desired eventuality to a powerful force. Justice, as we sadly learn, does not suffer manipulation.

When Justice's position indicates a negative meaning, we consider that she points out bias, intolerance, illegality, prejudice, misjudgment, or unevenness. When her position suggests a positive meaning, Justice offers adjustment, balance, lawfulness, objectivity, parity, recompense, or resolution.

Should the position of Justice suggest us or another person, her meaning is usually that of someone who is sitting in judgment or is in a position to promote or deny. If Justice indicates a circumstance, rather than a particular person, we expect to "pay the piper" in some way, possibly by being brought before the bench. In generic terms, the Justice card signals a need to recheck our thoughts or actions, to neutralize a negative influence from ourselves or others, or to prevent any further accumulation of karmic potential.

The appearance of Justice reversed often means a resolution comes in an unexpected form or is somehow thwarted. If a person is indicated, the reversal shows someone who is inappropriately judging, refusing to judge, or should back away from judgment.

As explained before, our greatest downfall in drawing upon Justice is our personal perspective. We must divest ourselves of preconceived conclusions and self-righteousness. No matter how much we distort her archetypal image to make her as blind to the truth as we are ourselves, Justice is the same for everyone. Until we acknowledge this dispassionate force of consciousness, we place ourselves in the scales of Justice and are weighed in the balance.

Magic in
the Cards

by Janina Renée

Sometimes you get an auspicious tarot reading that shows good energies at work in your life, or promises happy times to come, so you want to ride that wave and carry the good energy forward. Fortunately, in addition to the common sense sorts of things you can do to improve your luck, there are simple ritual actions you can perform to spark magic, based on symbols in your cards.

When you bring symbols from your tarot readings into everyday life—even in a superficial manner—you create a circuit of energy that sets magic in motion. Amplifying the cards' images can also bring out the best potentials of cards that come up reversed (indicating that their energies need help achieving fuller expression), or that are surrounded by cards of frustration. Such rituals can even help you come to terms with cards you find troubling: once their warnings are understood and acknowledged, you can consciously transform the images to soften their emotional impact.

Depending on how the cards in your reading lend themselves to symbolic gestures, you can build your rituals around one focal card, or a select group of cards, or you can find ingenious ways to combine all of the symbols in your layout.

When a reading speaks to you in a positive way, you can treat it as a tarot spell: pick up each card and visualize yourself carrying out the actions or experiencing the conditions that the cards portray, however they apply to your situation. You may also come up with affirmations to accompany the visualizations. Such a layout can be displayed as an altar arrangement surrounded by flowers, candles, and gemstones, and you can preserve it by mounting the cards on a cardboard background and framing it. If you don't want to sacrifice your cards, scan them or copy them. You can have creative fun with this by gluing beads, feathers, crystals, sequins, and bits of filigree around the edges.

A certain number of tarot cards are "people" cards, depicting distinctive personalities, such as the Magician, High Priestess, Empress, etc., and all of the court cards, so an effective way of activating these cards is to seek out the company of people who embody those qualities, since they can show us how to model these archetypes in our own lives. If you find it challenging to manage certain situations, and you draw a card depicting a skillful character, you can try to go through the day acting in his or her "mode." Ask yourself, for example, "What would the Hierophant do in this situation?"

One of the easiest ways to render the cards' symbolism more visible to your deep mind is to create altar arrangements, wall displays, crafts projects, or larger "art installations," decorated with symbols or physical objects portrayed in the cards. Because they use basic sets of material objects, the Minor Arcana readily lend themselves to this. Thus, if you get the Nine of Cups, representing the proliferation of emotional riches, you could set out nine fancy goblets. Or, as the Cups correspond to the Hearts in ordinary card decks, you could use this alternative symbolism, making a quilted wall hanging with nine calico hearts. With the Wands cards, one can

make garden arrangements by erecting staves or stakes in the number of your focal card. Paint them with bright colors and designs, and attach feathers, ribbons, beads, and pendants. Ropes or ribbons can be used to link these stakes in geometric patterns.

Displays can be enhanced by objects that correspond to the suits' emblems, such as coins, balls, round ornaments, beads, and stones for Pentacles; bottles, pots, vases, hearts, roses, and sea shells for Cups; pins, nails, scissors, thorns, feathers (representing the softer aspects of elemental Air), and spade-shaped leaves for Swords; and incense sticks, twigs, and acorns for Wands. (The acorns, spade-shaped leaves, and roses are used as suit symbols in various European card sets.)

The Major Arcana offers even more diverse possibilities. The Sun, Moon, and Star suggest decorations using glittering star garlands and tinsel, glow-in-the-dark planet cut-outs, and even Christmas lights in celestial shapes. If the appearance of the Death card has thrown a scare into you, you can tame the image of the Grim Reaper by making an arrangement with comical skull and skeleton figures. Celebrate "the Fool within" with clown, harlequin, or jester dolls. As the background and incidental symbols in cards can sometimes take on personal significance, these too can be featured in displays.

Choice of clothing is another way to align yourself with the symbolism of a particular card. Though most garments depicted in tarot cards would be hard to find, the cards offer some ideas you can use, and if they are too outlandish to wear in public, you might be able to dress up in the privacy of your home. For example, to honor the Magician or Strength, you could wear a broad-brimmed hat, as older tarot decks often portray them in hats whose shape suggests the lemniscate, which is both an infinity sign and symbolic of their mastery of solar and lunar forces. One can find pendants or other pieces of jewelry with emblematic shapes: Sun, Moon, stars, swords, coins, a lion for Strength, an eagle for the Emperor, and so on. To bring out the playful qualities of the Fool, wear Mardi Gras beads—especially ones with little jester heads on them. For men, it might be possible to find novelty ties imprinted with certain symbols. You can also choose clothing based on the colors in which your cards' characters are depicted, or other color cues in their images. For example, in the *Marseille* deck, different characters wear red and blue to denote combinations of active and passive energies.

Whether for altar decorations or jewelry, you may find certain gemstones have affinities with certain cards. So, in the case of the Fool, one can use pyrite, known as "Fool's gold," to assert that we all have the right to glitter now and then, even when we don't feel totally authentic. One could also use green aventurine; punning on its name, it signifies growth through adventure (in Italian, "*a ventura*" means "accidentally").

At this point, we can see the amuletic possibilities. In addition to carrying specific cards as talismans, one can use gemstones, emblematic jewelry, and related objects. These can be combined in charm bundles, such as the Haitian-style "Pacquet Congo," which is a cloth bag enclosing sacred earth and other magical media, and which can be quite a work of art when decorated with beads and feathers.

Beyond decoration, display, and talismanic uses, there are many possibilities for ritual action. Simple rituals can involve the manipulation of symbolic objects, as is often done in folk magic. For example, when the Nine of Swords reveals that you have been agonizing about things over which you have little control, transform the Swords' symbolism into something airier by making a "Witch's ladder"—a traditional form of which is a cord of nine knots and feathers. Identify nine worries, assigning one to each of your feathers. Take your time, as going over your worries gives you a chance to think about them objectively. Then, hang the cord from the branch of a tree with an invocation to the four winds to dissipate your cares.

Here's another example: popular depictions of the Two of Cups show a man and a woman coming together, holding two goblets up to each other. If this card comes up in relation to queries as to whether love or friendship will come into your life, you can magically help it happen by setting two goblets at some distance apart from each other and each day moving them a little closer together, while saying affirmations like, "My heart is open to love and friendship. Each day brings more opportunities to meet the right person." You could fill the two cups with water with a drop of anise extract in it as an offering to our friends in spirit, or you could use two cuplike candle holders with candles in them.

Indeed, candle-burning rites are well suited to improvised rituals, using candles corresponding to numbered cards. The Wands cards are associated with the fire element, so, in the case of the Eight of Wands (which shows how the organization of ideas and energies speeds us toward our goals), you could make an arrangement of eight pillar candles in warm colors. On the other hand, some systems associate the Swords with fire, so to deal with the issues in the Ten of Swords, which is about cycles of conflict, you could burn ten candles, together or in succession, with affirmations that as the candles burn your troubles diminish. Of course, candles can help activate the symbolism of those suits that aren't associated with fire, as in the example of the two cuplike candle holders mentioned above, and candles can be set out on pentacles. Novelty candles can also be put to use. Thus, a devil-shaped candle, which one might get in a Halloween store, could be burned while reciting affirmations for ridding oneself of bad habits represented by the Devil card—though for a person suffering from low energy, it could be used to signal a need to light up the libido.

Some cards' images suggest exercises used in ceremonial magic. So, to amplify the Ace of Sword's energy, you could use a blade to draw an invoking pentagram in the air (starting at the tip of the star and moving downward from right to left). Visualize the pentagram traced in white light, or in colored light appropriate to your goal. Visualize the Ace of Swords within that pentagram as a way of redoubling its imagery, or visualize yourself confidently pursuing your goals.

Many of the cards suggest activities involving food and drink. The possibilities for Cups are obvious. To activate the Pentacles cards, set good things out on plates, as in its most basic definition a pentacle is a type of plate. Because the Six of Pentacles denotes a stage of life in which you can share with others, you could invite friends over for a buffet consisting of six platters heaped with food. If you draw the Moon, you can affirm the revitalizing powers of the unconscious by filling a goblet with milk and taking it out under the night sky. (This will work best when a Full or near-Full Moon is riding high.) Lift the goblet, tilting it so moonlight can play on its surfaces, and make a toast, saying something like, "Lady Moon, I honor your mystery as I imbibe your power. Let this drink refresh the wild places in my spirit!" You could also honor the Moon's connection with the deep with a seafood dinner.

Sometimes cards may suggest more extended courses of action, such as going on an excursion. If you draw the Chariot, which is about being in control of your life, you could plan a trip where you are in charge of the driving and other details. In the case of the Hermit, you could act on its background symbolism, going to the mountains for a spiritual retreat.

Now that some tarot artists are breaking with tradition and exploring alternative images for cards, you have more options as a ritualist. For example, although most decks associate the Sevens with images of struggle, the *Witches Tarot* (by Reed and Cannon) highlights the innovative potentials of the Sevens by portraying a painter on the Seven of Wands and a group of musicians on the Seven of Swords.

While the suggestions offered here are very basic, your own tarot readings will provide ideas for more complexly layered symbols and activities. Actions based on card symbolism are most effective when you can find personalized ways to apply them.

Special Day Rituals

by Nina Lee Braden

S pecial days can be happy; special days can be sad. No matter what kind of special day you have, sometimes a tarot ritual will help you to either celebrate it or gain peace about it. A tarot ritual is not a tarot reading, although a ritual can include a reading. Lots of tarotists like to do a birthday reading for themselves. I do, and I highly recommend the practice. Others like to do readings for New Year's, anniversaries, or other special dates. I also encourage this habit. It occurs to me, though, that there might be a use for a special-day ritual, one that could be used for birthdays but also for special personal days such as anniversaries or other important dates—even special sad days. Some examples of special personal days: a Twelve-step "birthday," a spiritual dedication day, an initiation anniversary, the anniversary of the death of a loved one, a postdivorce wedding anniversary, or the birthday of an estranged friend or relative.

This is a group special-day ritual, but it can easily be performed by one person.

In honor of the chosen special day, choose a mutually convenient time. Allow time enough so that there is no pressure to rush. What is your special day? Is it a birthday? Is it an anniversary of some kind? Is it a sad day for you? No one outside of your group

has to know about your special day—that it is important to you is all that counts. If you wish, you may combine a special-day tarot reading as a part of this exercise, or you may choose to do a reading separately or not at all.

A Place for Magic

Since this is a special day for you, set the stage. Clear a space and decorate it. The space can be as small or as large as you like. If you have a regular ritual space that you use, you may adapt it for this ritual. The main thing is to designate the space in some way to reflect your special day. Is your special day a birthday? If so, decorate it with a birthday motif. Is your special day an anniversary? If so, decorate it to reflect the event that you are celebrating the anniversary of. Is it a day of sorrow? If so, you may decorate it in mourning colors or you may decorate it in symbols of peace and release, depending on your personal goals. Since this is a tarot ritual, be sure to include some tarot cards as a part of your decoration. You might choose some cards ahead of time and decorate in the colors predominant in those cards. You could draw or color your own cards or make some enlargements of cards to use as part of your decoration.

The important thing is to mark your space as different for this day. For this ritual, the space has a new function, and it should uniquely reflect the meaning of your special day. Your decoration can be as simple or as elaborate as you like. You may even wish to use robes or costumes. There is no need to be elaborate; be simple or complex—whichever pleases you.

Your ritual space need not be large, but it should have a table or altar big enough to hold the following items:

- Talismans representing your special day, such as photographs, mementos, symbols, or jewelry
- A deck of tarot cards
- Separate tarot cards (hand-colored or from a separate deck) that represent the special day

- Representation of the four elements—you may use the Aces from a second tarot deck
- Candles
- Something to represent cleansing, such as bells, censers, smudge wands, fans, salt water, or brooms
- Room for a small layout of tarot cards (or a second small table for this purpose)
- Pad and writing implement

Ritual Procedures

There are five officers in this ritual: one for each of the four elements plus the celebrant. If you are doing the ritual by yourself, you perform all five parts, simply changing the pronouns "you" and "your" to "I" and "my."

Air enters the sacred space, fanning or blowing the space to purify it, saying, "By the element of air, I cleanse and consecrate this sacred space." Air makes a circle, and then places the tool of cleansing on the altar. Fire enters the sacred space, carrying a candle or lamp, saying, "By the element of fire, I cleanse and consecrate this sacred space." Fire makes a circle, and then places the tool of cleansing on the altar. Water enters the sacred space, sprinkling water or other liquid around the space to purify it, saying, "By the element of water, I cleanse and consecrate this sacred space." Water makes a circle, and then places the tool of cleansing on the altar. Earth enters the sacred space, sprinkling salt or other dust-like granules around the space to purify it, saying, "By the element of earth, I cleanse and consecrate this sacred space." Earth makes a circle, and then places the tool of cleansing on the altar.

Others enter the circle at this time.

Earth: "This circle has been cleansed and consecrated by all four elements. Let all have peace, trust, and love in their hearts on this special day. The circle is now complete."

Air: "We come together today to celebrate (or mourn, or whatever term is most appropriate) _____ (name of special day)."

Earth: "We will remember the past."

Fire: "We will look to the future."

Water: "We will join in heart as we celebrate (or gain peace)."

Air: "Let us listen to the tarot's wisdom today."

Fire: "Let us feel the fire of tarot's inspiration."

Water: "Let us know in our hearts the message of the tarot."

Earth: "Let us honor the past through the tarot."

Celebrant goes through the deck, faceup, looking for a card that sums up the past meaning of this special day. It can be a happy card or a sad card, a card of peace or a card of turmoil. If there is trouble choosing one card that sums up the past meaning of the day, three may be chosen.

Celebrant places the card on the altar, stating how the card speaks to the past memory of the day. The celebrant should feel free to be brief or lengthy, as so moved. (If desired, Air can record notes of the celebrant's comments, and others in the circle may add comments after any response by the celebrant if they wish.)

Earth: "How does this card represent your past and this special day?"

Celebrant responds.

Water: "How does this card represent your emotions?"

Celebrant responds.

Fire: "How does this card represent your spiritual goals?"

Celebrant responds.

Air: "How does this card represent knowledge that you have gained?"

At this point, the celebrant may, if desired, do a reading for the special day. He or she should put the cards back into the deck and shuffle, and he or she should use a spread of personal choice. The celebrant may keep quiet his or her thoughts on the reading or may talk to the circle. Air may take notes. When the celebrant is done, the people portraying the elements comment:

Air: "Hold a mirror to this reading. What does the mirror reveal that your eyes do not? Hold a magnifying glass to the reading. What does the magnification reveal?"

Celebrant responds.

Fire: "Hold a flame to this reading to temper it. What does tempering reveal to you about this reading? Heat the reading up so that it sizzles, almost bursting into flame. What does this heat reveal to you about the reading?"

Celebrant responds.

Water: "Wash the reading. What does cleansing reveal to you about this reading? Saturate the reading with water. What does immersion in deep waters reveal to you about this reading?"

Celebrant responds.

Earth: "Ground this reading in practicality. What does this reading mean mundanely? How can you apply it to your daily life? What concrete changes in your life should you make? What one step can you make today to begin this change?"

Celebrant responds.

Next (whether or not the celebrant has done a reading), the celebrant should go through the tarot deck once again, faceup. He or she should choose one card to be a talisman for the next year. He or she may choose the same card that began the ritual or a different card.

The celebrant describes how he or she plans to use the card as a talisman in the year to come.

Air: "Let this card guide your thoughts for the year to come, letting you think clearly, wisely, and well."

Fire: "Let this card guide your passions for the year to come, letting your passions be true, honest, and pure.

Water: "Let this card guide your feelings for the year to come, letting your heart be warm and generous both to yourself and others."

Earth: "Let this card guide you physically, practically, and materially for the year to come. Balance noble goals, aspirations, and desires with the limitations of your body and other resources. Let it guide you to meet all of your needs, bodily and otherwise."

Air: "All elements are good, but any one element out of

balance with the other three can be detrimental to your personal development."

Fire: "Celebrate this special day fully, but do not become unbalanced."

Water: "Feel your emotions fully, but do not neglect your other needs."

Air: "This day and every day, may you walk like the Fool, pay attention like the Magician, remember like the High Priestess, embrace like the Empress, and rule like the Emperor."

Fire: "May you hold life together like the Hierophant, and discriminate like the Lovers. May you have the focus of the Chariot, and the controlled passion of Strength."

Water: "May you guide like the Hermit and be your own Wheel of Good Fortune. May you always be Just and Hang upside down until enlightened."

Earth: "May you Die daily through transformation and be Tempered into a perfect vessel."

Air: "May you laugh with the Devil and destroy your personal Towers of pretension."

Fire: "May the Star grant your wishes as you walk under the Moon and the Sun."

Water: "Let the call of the Judgment horn find you ready to dance in a new World."

Earth: "So mote it be. Thanks be for the blessings and guidance of the tarot today and every day."

Earth picks up the tool of earth from the altar and goes around the circle, saying, "I thank the element of earth for its presence in this ritual and in our lives. Blessed be the element of earth." Water picks up the tool of water from the altar and goes around the circle, saying, "I thank the element of water for its presence in this ritual and in our lives. Blessed be the element of water." Fire picks up the tool of fire from the altar and goes around the circle, saying, "I thank the element of fire for its presence in this ritual and in our lives. Blessed be the element of fire." Air picks up the tool of air from the altar and goes around the circle, saying, "I thank the element of air for its presence in this ritual and in our lives. Blessed be the element of air. Many thanks to all who have joined with us today. The circle is now open but never broken."

Attendees exit the circle, and then return to put away ritual articles.

A Closer Look At:

The Celtic Dragon Tarot

Created by D.J. Conway and Lisa Hunt

- 78 full-color cards and a 216-page illustrated book

- Cards are 4¾ x 2¾, with nonreversible backs and illustrated pips

- Delicate images and soft color palette evoke the fantasy art of Alan Lee and Jane Yolen

- Companion book emphasizes magical spell-working and meditation

- Deck and book contain spreads and techniques designed specifically for the *Celtic Dragon Tarot*

Four of Cups

5- high priest

17- The Star

1- The Magician

Eight of Pentacles

Working With Shadows

by Christine Jette

Editor's Note: This article is an expansion of the concept first presented in Ms. Jette's book Tarot and Shadow Work *(Llewellyn 1999).*

When I finished the manuscript for *Tarot Shadow Work* in 1999, I didn't believe I could write one more thing about tarot and the shadow. I was wrong. Time has passed and I am able to revisit the book with a more objective viewpoint. I originally wrote that I used only the twenty-two cards of the Major Arcana because shadow work is a spiritual endeavor. While this is true, it's time for authorial honesty: the concept of using seventy-eight cards eluded me in the beginning. Six years later, I know how to use an entire tarot deck when doing shadow work and the *Tarot Reader* is the perfect place to share my expanded ideas on shadow work.

Taking my cue from astrology, the Major Arcana cards represent the **what** of shadow work—a description of the shadow and what its challenges and gifts entail. The court cards are the **how** and **who** of shadow work—how the shadow presents itself in personality development and whom we draw to us for our life lessons. The Minor Arcana depict the **where** of shadow work, or in what department of life the shadow is operating.

The Major Arcana, the Fool through the World, speak to you of both life lessons and life wisdom: the qualities being tested and developed, your gifts and challenges, karma and the reasons you are here. The twenty-two cards symbolize spiritual development and help you understand your place in the world. The "Greater Secrets" will point to the higher overview of life and give you insights into the "big picture." They will also hint at your healing potential and what lies in the shadows. (See the appendix in *Tarot Shadow Work* for more information.)

The Minor Arcana, or "lesser secrets," offer information along the planes of existence: Wands, spiritual creativity in everyday life; Cups, emotions and feelings; Swords, psychological well being/the mind; and Pentacles, physical reality and the body.

When the different suits show up in a reading, ask yourself: What action can I take? (Wands) What am I feeling or dreaming about? (Cups) What am I thinking or what decision needs to be made? (Swords) Because Pentacles explore issues of food, housing, money, work, the body and physical health, ask yourself: What do I value?

In life, there is no separation between body, emotion, mind, and spirit. It is impossible for something to happen to us without all four levels of existence being affected. It is likewise impossible to change without attending to these same four levels of being. Life does not fall neatly into categories. Because stress or concerns at any level affect all levels, the lines sometimes blur.

No other cards in the tarot deck have more interpretations than the court cards. Just pick up any three tarot books and compare. It's mind-boggling. We all have qualities that are traditionally associated with both masculine and feminine ways of being—for instance, a woman can be competitive and a man can be nurturing. So be aware that the King and Knight can represent a woman and the Queen can symbolize a man. The gender or "occupation" of the court card is less important than the qualities it describes.

Pages can represent a child, but they also introduce the element of their suits, the willingness to change, take a risk, or learn something new. Pages can symbolize the catalyst needed for change and the child within us all. Pages also carry messages related to their suits: telephone calls or significant e-mail (Page of Wands); important dreams (Page of Cups); written warnings (Page of Swords); and, messages from your body, especially in the form of illness (Page of Pentacles).

Knights represent young adults or people who are starting over, focusing on a specific task through their suits, whether creative (Wands), emotional (Cups), psychological (Swords), or physical (Pentacles). Our "knightly" qualities include being energetic, daring, headstrong, and goal-oriented. Knights show movement and action through their suits.

Queens are mature. They take their understanding of life inward and use this life wisdom to nurture others and encourage self-development through their specific suits: the Queen of Cups nurtures the emotions, the Queen of Swords attends to mental health, and the fiery Queen of Wands engages the sagging spirit. Because they are the embodiment of the feminine tradition of healing, Queens often represent healing in relationship to their suit. An example of this is the Queen of Pentacles symbolizing a natural healer. Our "queenly" qualities include sensitivity, fullness of expression, empathy, and inner control.

Kings are also mature, but they project their maturity outward in the form of leadership through their suits. They take charge and give advice: creative or spiritual advice (King of Wands); emotional advice (King of Cups); psychological or intellectual advice (King of Swords); and practical advice about the everyday world (King of Pentacles, especially in the area of finances or work). Our "kingly" qualities include being capable and in control, with an air of authority, leadership, and worldliness.

So how do you use the entire deck in shadow work? It's simple. Separate your deck into three stacks: the twenty-two Majors, forty Minors and sixteen court cards. Do a star layout, or any other tarot activity in *Tarot Shadow Work* using Majors only, as described in the book. Look at your shadow layout or activity and select one card that puzzles or bothers you, or one that you especially like. Pull that card out of the layout.

Now think of the Minor Arcana and court cards as the cards to use for more information. Shuffle your Minor card stack. As you shuffle, concentrate on **where**, or in what department of life, this particular Major card is operating. For example, you have chosen the Fool from the shadow layout because you know you allow others to take advantage of you and have decided this most needs work now. The Minor card that turns up is the Ten of Wands.

You first decide if the Ten of Wands describes the challenge of the shadow or the gift of the shadow. In other words, does the card feel negative or positive? Hint: If you like the card, it probably represents a gift of shadow work, something to keep and nurture. If it feels negative, it means it is a lesson to be learned, something to improve or work on. You realize that it depicts the challenge of the shadow: others take advantage of you because you are unable to say no and you take on too much responsibility as a result.

As you shuffle the court card stack, concentrate on **how** the shadow presents itself in your personality. You can also think about the people in your life and why they might be there. Remember, the court cards are *always* a reflection of you—you draw the people to you that you need for your life wisdom. So it doesn't matter if the court card describes someone else. The card is still about you and your need to have those qualities in your life for good or ill. Randomly select one court card. First decide if it represents the shadow's challenge or the shadow's gift. Does it feel negative or positive to you?

Continuing with our example, you have drawn the Queen of Pentacles. At first you think, "Oh, great, the smothering mother card." After some thought, you decide she symbolizes the shadow's gift after all: Yes, you have been taken advantage of because of your need to nurture (rescue) others; but the answer is still in the Queen of Pentacles—if you start saying no and allow others to learn self-responsibility. Then they are able to find their own ways, and you are free of the martyr's shadow.

You can use the Minor and court cards for more information on any shadow star layout, single card in a layout, or any tarot activity in the book. Using the entire deck helps pinpoint both strengths and challenges of doing shadow work. Think of it as your magnifying mirror for a better reflection of you. And for goodness sake, trust your intuition when deciding if a card feels negative or positive. Only you can know that. To review, ask the following questions when doing shadow work with the entire deck:

- For Major Arcana cards: **what** shadow is this card describing? Does this card symbolize the challenge of shadow work or the reward for facing the shadow, the gift of shadow work?

- For Minor Arcana cards: **where**, or in what department of life is this card operating? (Physical, financial, emotional, psychological, legal, creative, or spiritual pursuits, etc., according to its suit.) Is this card a challenge (something that needs work) or something to keep and nurture?

- For court cards: **how** does the shadow present itself in my personality development? **how** do other people see me? **how** do I see myself? **whom** have I drawn into my life for soul development? Does this card describe the shadow's challenge or gift?

For me, shadow work and its resulting soul development are meaningless if not viewed through the lens of everyday living. Divinity lies in the details of life. The magic of shadow work doesn't come from the tarot cards—the magic comes from our willingness to change. If we ascribe to the philosophy of "as above, so below," then who we are and what we do is spirituality in action—not "out there" somewhere, but in us, here and now. May you find joy in the shadows.

World to World
Tarot and Kabbalah
by Rachel Pollack

Over the centuries of spiritual interest in the tarot, people have suggested many traditions and concepts to which we can link the cards. By far the most popular and accepted of these is the very complex system of ideas and images known as Kabbalah. Kabbalah (a Hebrew word which means "received," as in a teaching received directly from a master to an initiate) goes back at least two thousand years, to some of the earliest rabbis. In the late Middle Ages/early Renaissance—exactly the same period as the first known tarot decks—Kabbalah began to move from a strictly Jewish teaching into the wider European "Hermetic" tradition (named for a mysterious God-like figure named Hermes Trismegistus, who was said to compose the earliest Hermetic texts—around the same time, in fact, as some of the earliest texts in Kabbalah). The links many people know today between tarot and Kabbalah belong to the tradition known as Western Kabbalah—a blend of Jewish, Christian, and Pagan mystical ideas and images.

The links between tarot and Kabbalah are largely structural. The central image of Kabbalah (especially Western Kabbalah) is a symbol known as the Tree of Life, after the Tree that stood in the center of the Garden of Eden. This Tree consists of ten circles of divine energy, called *sephiroth* (plural of *sephirah*, a Hebrew word that

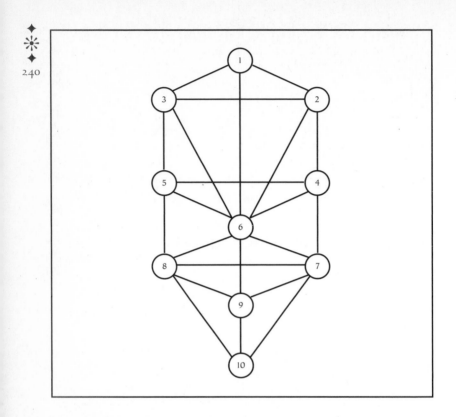

derives from sapphire), along with twenty-two connecting lines. Each of these twenty-two lines belongs to a letter in the Hebrew alphabet, with all the symbolic, philosophical, and mystical meanings that go with each one of those ancient letters. As all tarotists know, there are twenty-two cards in the highly symbolic and mystical "Major Arcana" of the tarot. It becomes possible, therefore, to match the Major cards with the lines of the Tree, and the Hebrew letters, and all the deep symbolic meanings and correspondences that belong to them. The pattern of the Tree is shown above, with the most common version (there are many) of the twenty-two lines.

But what of the ten sephiroth, which after all are the basic form of the Tree? The tarot contains four suits, and each suit contains cards Ace through Ten, so that we can actually lay the cards out in the form of the Tree itself. This correspondence becomes even stronger when we learn that Kabbalah teaches of not one Tree, but four. The four Trees symbolize what Kabbalists call the four worlds of existence, just as the four tarot suits represent the four "elements," fire, water, air, and earth. Each of these four worlds goes on all the time. There's the physical world that we can see and touch, but there's also the mental world that goes on in our minds, and the world of our emotions, and the world of high principles or spirituality. At any moment we might be conscious of one of these "worlds" more than another, but they all exist. Kabbalah, and tarot, help us recognize them.

Most of the time, when we learn of the possible connections between tarot and the Tree of Life we give our attention to how they illuminate each other. In other words, we examine the particular correspondences between, say, the highest point on the Tree, the top sephirah, known as *Kether* or Crown, and the first card of each suit, the Ace. Here are the names of the ten sephiroth, in order, with a very brief description of their meaning. By necessity, we will have to keep these meanings very simple. For those who want a fuller exploration of the sephiroth, please see my book *The Kabbalah Tree*.

1) *Kether*—Crown: highest potential, greatest possibility; the Ace of each suit.

2) *Hokhmah*—Wisdom: a person's greatest truth, the wisdom we find in our lives or in a particular moment; the Two of each suit.

3) *Binah*—Understanding: how we use that truth in our lives; the Three of each suit.

4) *Chesed*—Mercy: our gifts, the wondrous qualities of our lives; the four of each suit.

5) *Gevurah*—Power: the challenges and difficulties that shape us and teach us; the Five of each suit.

6) *Tiferet*—Beauty: the center of the Tree, and so the center, or core of our lives, or who we are at a particular moment; the Six of each suit.

7) *Netzach*—Victory, also called Eternity: the sphere of love and emotion; the Seven of each suit.

8) *Hod*—Glory: the sphere of intellect; the Eight of each suit.

9) *Yesod*—Foundation: the imagination, or the unconscious, the place of dreams and creativity; the Nine of each suit.

10) *Malkuth*—Kingdom: the outer world and its effect on us; the influence of events, or other people; the Ten of each suit.

Now that we have some small sense of the sephiroth, we need to consider the differences between the worlds. The simplest way is to link these to the four elements that go with each suit. In the most common version, these are:

Wands—fire—inspiration—movement

Cups—water—emotion—imagination

Swords—air—mind—awareness—conflicts

Pentacles—earth—material things—work—practical issues

The four worlds of Kabbalah actually carry somewhat different meanings, so you might want to focus on the more Kabbalistic approach as you travel from world to world. Here are the Kabbalistic titles, their English translations, and very basic meanings:

Atzilut—Emanation—the world of pure essence. The highest truth. We can connect this to Wands and fire.

Beriah—Creation—the world in which truth begins to take on distinct shape, and clarity. A student in one of my classes referred to Beriah as "the primordial soup." On a personal level, we can think of it as the unconscious. This world is still in movement, or flux, and so we can link it to Cups, the element of water.

Yetsirah—Formation—this is the world of definite ideas and principles, in which we see clearly. Yetsirah is the world of consciousness. We can compare this to the element of air, and so the suit of Swords.

Assiyah—Action—the world of events, of physicality, what we think of as "the real world." We can link it to Pentacles, and the element of earth.

Notice that some of the ten sephiroth share qualities with a particular world. Atzilut is similar to Kether (and Hokhmah); Beriah perhaps to Netzach, or Yesod; Yetsirah to Hod; and Assiyah to Malkuth. The symbols shift and overlap, but each world gives its own special quality to the ten sephiroth.

But the tarot carries a very special quality itself. Though we number the cards, and visualize their structure, they do not actually come in a fixed pattern. Instead, we hold them in our hands as a pack of cards. And we can mix those cards, shuffle them, and see what new patterns they form, or the ways in which they point us to new awareness. Through the simple method of doing readings, we actually can move about in the Tree of Life. We can discover our place in the Tree, or in each of the four Trees of the four worlds, at any particular moment.

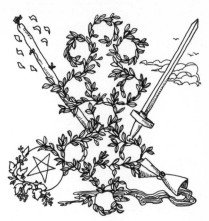

The following reading allows us to do just that: look at where we find ourselves in each world, and what issue we face there, and how to approach it. You can do this sitting at your table, the same as any reading, but the Tree is such a powerful visual symbol that it gives us a chance to act out the reading as a ritual. In this way, we can physically journey to each world by laying out the cards in the corners of a room, with the Major Arcana, the cards of archetypal energies, in the center.

To do this reading you will need two tarot decks, and a space large enough to lay out all the cards on the floor. We will use the first deck to set out the Four Worlds. Set each suit out in the pattern of the Tree, all of them pointing to the center. You can lay them out in the four corners of the room, or else match them to the four compass points. Since different traditions assign different compass points to the suits I will simply show the cards in the corners. Feel free to change this to suit your own system.

When you have set out the four suits, arrange the Major Arcana in a circle, with the Fool and the World as outer points, and leave gaps or gates to move to each of the worlds. Finally, set the sixteen court cards in a pack in the center, as symbols of the many aspects of the self. The pattern should look like the one on the next page.

Now take the second deck of cards (you can use two of the same deck, or if you prefer, two different decks for contrast), and separate them into Major cards, cards Ace through Ten of each suit (you want each suit together—that is, all the Wands, all the Cups, etc.), and court cards. Do not separate the court cards by suit. Now you are ready to begin. You might want to take a small bell or a rattle to signify your symbolic movement into and out of each of the worlds.

Stand in the center of the circle, by the pack of court cards from the first deck. Take a few deep breaths, and sound the bell or rattle to give yourself the sense of standing in the very center of your

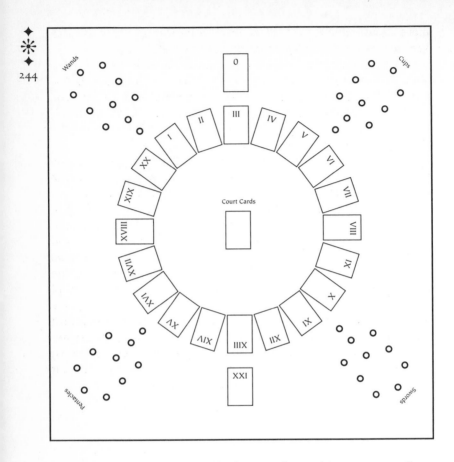

existence, the place from which everything else emerges. Allow yourself to experience being there before going on to the next step.

When you feel ready, exit the circle through the first gate, the one that points to the suit of Wands, the fire world of Atzilut. Stand at the foot of Malkuth, so you can look up the Tree, sephirah to sephirah from Malkuth to Kether. Sound the bell or rattle to signify your presence there. When you have taken some time to contemplate this world, shuffle the ten numbered Wands cards. Pull one card to tell you where you are in this world. If you happen to get the six, then you are in Tiferet in the world of Atzilut. Consider what it might mean to be in the very center, or core, of the world of pure essence, the world of fire.

Next shuffle the Major cards, and pull one to tell you what issue you face in this world. Try to think of the card not just in its usual meanings but in terms of the special qualities of that world or element. If you get the Wheel of Fortune in Atzilut it might mean karmic truth, rather than a current turn of events.

Finally, shuffle the sixteen court cards and pull one to show what quality or aspect of yourself you will need to deal with that issue in that world. When you have contemplated the cards you have received, replace the Major and court cards in their places, since they might show up again in one of the other worlds. The Wands card you can keep separate.

Now, take a deep breath and sound the bell or rattle to leave the first world. Return to the circle through the same gate, and take a moment to regain that quality of being in the center. When you feel ready, exit through the second gate, the one that points to Cups, and travel to the world of Beriah. Follow the same process as above, but now choose a single card from the Cups suit to show you where you are in the world of creation, of water. Return through the same gate.

Repeat the process for the final two worlds. Each time, imagine that you actually are traveling to these wondrous worlds, with all their different qualities. Let your imagination, and the cards, carry you from world to world. When you have returned for the fourth time to the center (after your journey to the earth world of Assiyah, as represented by the suit of Pentacles), close your eyes, sound the bell or rattle one more time, take a deep breath, and when you let it out release yourself from the ritual and the journey.

Judgment

Deck Reviews

The Baroque Bohemian Cats' Tarot

reviewed by Lee Bursten

When I first saw an online scan of a card from this deck, I immediately decided that I wouldn't touch it with a ten-foot pole. I like to think of myself as open-minded when it comes to gender roles, but as a man, I found the whole concept of cats dressed in fancy costumes to be so inherently feminine that it made me cringe inwardly, as I do when I walk through the lingerie section of the department store.

Fortunately, I took a second look. After all, I'm a cat person, having shared living quarters with various cats since childhood. After obtaining the deck and spending quite some time with it, it no longer seems particularly feminine. Cats themselves transcend human distinctions of gender roles, and the *Baroque Bohemian Cats' Tarot* does as well.

Karen Mahony and Alex Ukolov, the creative team behind the magical *Tarot of Prague*, have worked their sorcery a second time, producing an entrancing tarot experience. For the present deck, photographs of cats have been digitally combined with brilliantly colorful costumes (handmade for the deck by Anna Hakkarainen), and placed into varied settings, which include paintings, sculptures, and photographed rooms and buildings—all from the Czech Republic, where the artists reside.

THE STAR

The Star from *The Baroque Bohemian Cats' Tarot*

The vibrant and intricate images are a riot of color and form, yet the eye is kept focused on the central figure on each card. This deck is all about personality, and what sets it apart from other decks is the powerfully evocative way in which it communicates that personality by utilizing subtle, yet profound, variations in the cats' expressions, the breeds chosen for each card, and the postures and gestures of their bodies.

Despite the sharp photo-realism of the images, these cards don't really look as if someone actually dressed up cats in fancy costumes, thank goodness. The bodies of the cats have been cunningly altered by digital means so that they conform to the general contours of human bodies, while retaining paws and fur. The result is an anthropomorphized creature who looks very much like standard depictions of Puss 'n Boots.

Curiously, the substitution of feline figures for human ones tends to emphasize the humanity of the tarot archetypes. Perhaps we are simply desensitized to images of people sternly gazing back at us from their thrones. Certainly, replacing humans with animals allows the artists to indicate emotion and expression in a fresh and immediate way. The same effect can be seen in Angelo Giannini's *Tarot of the Animal Lords*, which depicts a different animal on each card. But the effect is heightened in the *Bohemian Cats* because cats' expressions and gestures can be so tantalizingly similar to our own. A good example is the Tower card, which shows two cats falling unceremoniously through the air. Anyone who has lived with a cat knows how very alarming it is to see such dignified creatures reduced to such undignified positions. But, as the accompanying book points out, the distressing qualities of the card (traditionally interpreted as disruptions and calamities) can be ameliorated by reminding oneself of a cat's ability to twist in midair and land on its feet after a fall—a skill which we would do well to emulate.

While this deck is certainly whimsical, I would categorize it as leaning towards the whimsy of absurdist literature rather than a merely frivolous whimsy. Mahony and Ukolov do not shy away from presenting the more negative sides of the cards. In fact, traditionally negative cards are particularly painful in this deck, due to the automatic sympathy most people will feel for animals who are in danger or suffering. At the same time, I appreciated the artists' willingness to include humorous or absurd elements in traditionally serious cards. Once I accepted the basic cats-in-costumes conceit, I was able to see the deck as one which takes itself seriously while retaining a healthy sense of humor about itself. I would challenge even the most humor-impaired occultist to examine these cards without cracking a smile—or bursting out laughing.

It turns out that there is a serious theme underlying the deck. I realize some readers may think this is like trying to find profound sociological significance in Mickey Mouse, but I'm convinced that the artists deliberately meant to address issues of power hierarchies—that is to say, the relationships between groups who hold differing kinds of power relative to each other.

THE MOON

The Moon from *The Baroque Bohemian Cats' Tarot*

THE DEVIL

The Devil from *The Baroque Bohemian Cats' Tarot*

THE TOWER

The Tower from The Baroque Bohemian Cats' Tarot

There are many cards in this deck that show humans lording it over cats, cats lording it over birds, and cats lording it over humans. In cards that traditionally show supernatural forces, the *Bohemian Cats* deck uses humans to represent those forces, which is quite appropriate, since one could reasonably assume that cats view humans warily, as capricious and unpredictable gods. For instance, the Devil card shows two cats chained to a tapestry of a human devil, and the Tower card shows a human god dislodging two cats from the tower by hurling thunderbolts. Other cards reverse the equation: the Chariot card shows a vehicle driven by a cat and pulled by two humans. Marionettes are featured on three cards, further reinforcing the power hierarchy theme.

My personal favorites include the gardener on the Seven of Pentacles, who takes an infectious pride in his crop; the Ten of Pentacles, whose elderly cat thoughtfully meditates on the success and security which surround him; and the Judgement card, whose humanoid angels have an amusingly businesslike air as they convey two apprehensive cats to their heavenly reward. I can just hear them saying, "Okay, who's next?"

I have only a few small cavils. On some cards, behind the main figure, the artists place an alternate image representing the same concept, in effect doubling the image. Personally I prefer tarot images to focus on a single figure or action, and I find the doubled image distracting. To be fair, though, there are readers who enjoy seeing a concept illustrated in different ways on the same card, and for those readers this feature would be a plus.

While the artists are ingenious at finding ways to clearly illustrate the cards' meanings, there are a few cards where it would be difficult for a novice reader to make out what's going on. Precise hand gestures (such as handing someone a coin) are tricky when it's a paw instead of a hand. But for those few instances where the cards don't shine forth with meaning, it's easy enough to consult the book, which makes everything crystal clear.

Although the deck is available separately without the book, I would strongly recommend purchasing the deck/book set. The paperback book by Karen Mahony is attractively produced, with pleasantly glossy pages, and, like the *Tarot of Prague*, includes many fascinating illustrations—including the original sources of much of the artwork shown on the cards. I particularly enjoyed reading about how some of the feline models actually exempli-

The Knight of Wands from *The Baroque Bohemian Cats' Tarot*

fied the qualities of the cards they were chosen for. Mahony makes connections to cats in myth and literature, as well as to how cats actually behave in real life. Two spreads are included, with sample readings. I particularly liked the "Cat's Tale" spread, which is designed so that certain card positions are to be read with the book's meanings, while for the other card positions we are encouraged to intuitively interpret the pictures.

Mahony has a talent for laying things out in a clear, uncomplicated, and unpretentious way—an ideal approach for a beginner. But even experienced tarotists will find much to interest them in this book. Each page contains surprising and pithy insights, not only to these particular images but to the tarot in general.

My biggest consideration when evaluating any deck is how well it reads. These cards speak (or meow) very loudly and clearly. Despite the intricate and elaborate nature of the artwork, the postures and expressions of the cats seem to leap across the gap between the cards and my brain, and I immediately grasp where that card fits into the story I'm telling. And in a different reading, that same card will communicate a different meaning just as loudly and clearly. This makes the reading process easy and enjoyable; ironic, when one considers that cats are often seen as mysterious and uncommunicative.

■
✳
■

Much as I enjoy this deck, I will have to admit that it's not for everyone. I suspect some people will just not be able to accept the cats-in-frilly-costumes thing. But to anyone who is reading this and thinks they would never, ever get this deck, I would say this: Never say never. If you detect within yourself the tiniest glimmer of attraction to this deck, then go ahead and have a second look. You'll be glad you did.

Tarot
of the Dead

reviewed by Errol McLendon

In my opinion, there are two basic types of decks: practical decks to be used in readings, meditations, and spell work, and art decks to be collected because they are aesthetically pleasing. My first impression of *Tarot of the Dead/Tarot de los Muertos* (all printing in the "little white book," or LWB, and on the cards is in both Spanish and English) was that it was a unique art deck; however, now that I have lived and read with the deck over the past week, I believe it is a very powerful practical deck as well. Part of my misinterpretation of the deck evolves from its 1960s comic-book style of illustration coupled with its wry sense of humor, but to fully appreciate this deck, one must view it through the eyes of the culture that inspired the deck's creation.

In Mexico, the Day of the Dead, usually celebrated in early November, is a time when the dead are honored—but not in a morbid North American "Memorial Day" style. Renowned writer Octavio Paz observes that, undaunted by death, the Mexican has no qualms about getting up close and personal with death, noting that he ". . . chases after it, mocks it, courts it, hugs it, sleeps with it; it is his favorite plaything and his most lasting love." In Mexico, the symbols of death are recreated in candy, puppets, papier-mâché figures, and toys. In this environment, the bones of our ancestors are not to be feared or mourned, but are to be invited out for lunch. In fact, picnics are held in cemeteries so that the spirits can enjoy a bit of the fun and festivities on this, their special day. Altars are set up in homes and include food and beverages; water and towels, so that the spirits may freshen up; cigarettes for deceased smokers (it can't really hurt anything now); and toys and candy for the spirits of children. In any Mexican market, even here in the United States, there are entire sections devoted to the folk art of the human skeleton.

To fully appreciate this deck, one must learn to relax into the celebration of death. The creator of the deck states it best when she says "The shadow of mortality makes the minor worries of the day silly, petty, and ridiculous. It throws into sharp contrast what is important, or even that nothing is all that important." By laughing at and with death, we begin to put other elements of our lives into perspective.

And laugh I did. Monica Knighton has a wicked sense of humor. A few examples will give you an idea of the giggles one might be surprised to find in a deck about death. The traditional Fool walks off a cliff, where our Dead Fool is hitchhiking accompanied by his skeletal dog. I believe hitchhiking carries the same fear of the unknown that this card is supposed to have. The Emperor's bony remains are dressed in a suit and seated in front of a huge old desktop computer, talking on an antiquated dial telephone, commanding to the end—and beyond. The Hierophant sits on his lawn accompanied by a mirror ball and two pink flamingos—"the conventions of society,"

0 The Fool
El Loco

The Fool from *Tarot of the Dead*

according to the LWB. My favorite is the Hanged Man, who has caught his head as it drops from his body. Though at first these images may seem slightly disturbing or disconnected, by spending some time with them, and the LWB, I believe you will love the world that Ms. Knighton has created.

Not all cards are humorous, though. I thought the Hermit, being led by a jar of fireflies, was inspired. Temperance is drawn as two skeletons joined at the pelvis, working to blend water from two separate cups. The Star card is absolutely gorgeous. Ms. Knighton has made few changes from the *Rider-Waite-Smith* Star card, with the exception that the nude figure is now much more than nude. There is something about the huge trees, parting clouds, and protective stars that make this card incredibly comforting. Finally, the Sun card, always one of my favorites, shows two skeletons in a desert setting, joining hands in a symbol of mutual respect and acceptance.

XIII

Death from *Tarot of the Dead*

257

The immediate question which must come to mind is, "What does the Death card look like in a death deck?" This is the most satisfying surprise of all. It is the only card that has a live person on it—and not only alive, but obviously pregnant, thus conveying the true meaning of card XIII: rebirth and transformation. In her wisdom, Ms. Knighton leaves this card unnamed. I found it interesting that the appearance of the only living person in seventy-eight cards had the same jarring effect as the one Death card has on me in a normal deck. Mission accomplished.

The suits are a bit different from a standard deck and I did have to rely on the LWB to help me follow Ms. Knighton's logic; however, once I understood the reason for her choices, I found them very appropriate and satisfying. I also liked the fact that the suits give this deck an overall feeling of a Sergio Leone spaghetti western. The suits are Pens (Wands), Coffins (Cups), Pistols (Swords), and Reels (Pentacles). Pens are the source of creativity, like a writer (or any creator) brainstorming and creating from an inspirational fire. Coffins represent funerals at which the living are allowed to deal with their emotions. The Pistols represents the same process of maintaining justice that Swords bring to mind. Finally, Reels represent the material world, but the use of a movie film reel as the symbol of the suit reminds us that our reality is filtered through our perception. Ms. Knighton does an excellent job of expanding on my brief explanations in her LWB.

The court cards are of the two-headed design usually seen in normal playing cards, but Ms. Knighton has made each of the two heads different. Her dry, humorous touch is evident here as well, giving one King of Coffins a banjo and a fedora while his buddy enjoys the music, martini in hand. One Page of Reels sports a baseball cap and carries a bat and ball, while his companion is wrapped in movie film and wears a hat made from newspaper. One Page of Pens stares through cat's-eye glasses at a fire he/she has just started, while a skeletal fire-breathing lizard crawls diagonally across this card. One should have no trouble telling these gentlemen and ladies apart.

King of Coffins
Rey de Ataúdes

The King of Coffins from *Tarot of the Dead*

My only minor disappointment is that the Minor Arcana are pip-only cards. Although I love the renderings of these cards, I can't help but wonder what Ms. Knighton could have done with the Ten of Pistols or the Five of Reels in a pictorial format. But this is a minor criticism of a wonderfully unique deck. Even the pip-type Minor Arcana cards surge with their own energy. The Pens glow and burst into flame, backed by an ever-changing background of diamonds and triangles; the Pistols are backed by crescent moons; the Reels rest on a yellow field broken by diamond shapes; and the Coffins rest on a calming green waterlike background. A new reader would definitely have trouble attributing meaning to these cards; however, they read wonderfully if you are on a more advanced level.

The *Tarot of the Dead* set comes with a black organdy bag and a cardboard storage box. There is also a card that shows a very interesting pyramid spread that offers two possible courses of action for a potential outcome. A more detailed explanation of this spread is also included in the LWB.

My opinion is that this is not a deck that should be glanced at casually in a store. Buy it. Take it home. Live with it. Have fun with it. Laugh with it. Take it out in November and share some time with departed friends. *Tarot of the Dead/Tarot de los Muertos* is a total blast. When it is my time to go to that great big Tarot Convention in the sky, I hope that someone will remember the spirit of this tarot deck and celebrate my death instead of lamenting it. Long live *Tarot de los Muertos*!

The Pagan Tarot

reviewed by Elizabeth Hazel

The Pagan Tarot, a Lo Scarabeo deck designed by artists Luca Raimonda and Cristiano Spadoni, with text by Rev. Gina M. Pace (a.k.a. Wicce) features depictions of contemporary pagan life in a seventy-eight-card format. The cards show scenes of a pagan, Wiccan, or Earth-based lifestyle, and does so by including the trappings of modern life for the twenty-first-century neophyte, initiate, or priest or priestess.

This deck strays from the classic *Rider-Waite-Smith* symbolism, with some haphazard departures in both the Major and Minor Arcanas. One may debate whether modernization increases or erodes the power of the archetypal models generally rendered in tarot art. In this deck, the modern settings and departures from mainstream tarot symbolism attempt to evoke additional meaning, as the cards require deeper study and consideration to plumb their meaning. Sometimes the artists are successful in this respect, but sometimes they are not. The "little white book" that accompanies the deck gives very brief meanings for the trump cards and court cards, but no explanatory information about the artwork. The numbered pip cards are detailed by number rather than by individual card meanings. The deck follows one of the more popular elemental orderings: Wands = Fire, Chalices = Water, Swords = Air, and Pentacles = Earth.

As is true with all Lo Scarabeo tarot decks, the name of the card is printed in five languages on the actual cards; the LWB contains a brief summary of the deck in English, Italian, Spanish, French, and German. Although this makes the *Pagan Tarot* accessible to an international spectrum of tarotists, it does limit the amount of useful information about the deck contained in the booklet. Because the booklet omits specific descriptions of the numbered (or pip) cards, it would be rather difficult for a beginner to use this deck without an additional source book. One hopes that a detailed book about the deck will be written, both to provide greater insights about the images on the trump cards and to give thorough details about the pip cards.

At first impression, some of the trump cards are clear and meaningful, while others are confusing or undecipherable without deeper study. For instance, in the Temperance card, a woman sits at a desk in an office, making an infinity symbol with her finger. She is drawing upon higher powers to inspire her work, blending the mystic with the mundane. But the Chariot requires some study. It depicts a woman seated on the bumper of a heavily packed parked car, with two men in the background. Why is the woman sitting? Are the men passengers or strangers approaching to offer assistance? The "little white book" (LWB) says about this card, " . . . we have felt as though our wheels were spinning getting us nowhere . . . we are about to begin to see our energies released for growth and movement again."

Elemental of Chalices from *The Pagan Tarot*

While many of the cards are evocative, some of the cards are better described as provocative. The Hierophant card shows people throwing books into a bonfire. This picture suggests one of the most extreme meanings for the Hierophant card: authority claiming the right to proscribe literature—and, by extension, thoughts—that they find unacceptable; and the use of force for suppression. This is not the only meaning (or even a central meaning) for the Hierophant card.

As far as I know, book burnings in the United States became passé after the McCarthy era ended, making this scene an anachronistic inclusion in a deck targeting contemporary pagans. The Judgement card also features images of past persecution rather than offering positive future choices or a spiritual awakening. While I do not care for decks that white-wash divinatory meanings, both the Judgement and Hierophant cards are extremely spiritual cards, and it was disappointing to see flashbacks to the burning times rather than positive contemporary role models.

The Six of Chalices from *The Pagan Tarot*

While some nudity is usual in tarot decks, collectors will find it more prevalent in decks designed by European artists. The Tower shows two naked couples engaging in explicit activity, and a robed initiate in the foreground with her back turned to them. The LWB says about this card, "If we do not relinquish the paths of baser nature; if we continue to act in ways that are not in our greatest good, the Tower tears down those things that are dangerous to us, and forces us to confront the reality before us." I am not convinced this design was the only way, or best way, to convey this point. Considering how very good some of the original trump designs are, there are a few trump designs that would have benefited from either better selection of the imagery or more extensive explanations in the LWB. Readers using this deck will need to spend time studying the artwork in order to contemplate their personal interpretations of the unusual and sometimes baffling images.

One of the most amusing examples of the Euro styling in this deck can be found in the Hermit card. It shows a young woman writing at her desk, and drawn at an angle that provides a clear view of the woman's décolletage. As far as I know, this is the first Hermit with a push-up brassiere. Since this accentuated cleavage line is almost exactly in the center of the composition, it distracts from the serious aspects of the drawing—the pentagram, athame, candles, and books that surround the woman working at her desk.

A unique design departure is the titling and arrangement of the court cards. The designations have been adjusted to reflect levels of pagan study: Novice (Knight), Initiate (Queen), and Elder (King). The court cards show additional modifications: Wands and Swords (yang elements) feature male figures, while the Chalices and Pentacles (yin elements) feature women. This is an innovative rebalancing of the court cards. They also show seasonal relationships: the Novice, Initiate, and Elder of Wands are depicted in a summer environment, Cups in spring, Pentacles in autumn, and Swords in winter.

The creatures representing Pages, the Elementals, are superb examples of fantasy art designs. The fiery Wand Elemental is a salamander; the Chalice Elemental is an undine; the Elemental of Pentacles is a wrinkled gnome; and the Elemental of Swords is a zephyr. These four cards are exquisitely rendered in both concept and execution, and are some of the most beautiful cards in the deck.

The numbered pip cards, Ace through Ten, show the numeric progress of each suit's element. Sometimes the central figure is solitary, generally a woman; other cards feature a group of practitioners, usually robed. The Wands, Chalices, and Swords include the suit's tools in the images—for example, the Four of Chalices shows a woman enjoying a solitary outdoor picnic with three cups in front of her and a single large chalice behind her. The Four of Wands shows a newly hand-fasted couple with four wands overhead. In the Six of Chalices, a woman watches her daughter have a tea party with her dolls; three tea cups are on the tea table, and three chalices above complete the numeric designation.

The Pentacle pip cards omit the pentacles on the numbered cards. However, the Pentacle pips are more evocative of day-to-day incidents, some quite humorous. In the Four of Pentacles, a young woman is choosing items from a grocery store shelf. In the Five of Pentacles, the same dark-haired young woman is waiting in a long line at a bank, with a man behind her putting his hand in her purse or inside of her coat—I couldn't decide if he was stealing or engaged in unsolicited fondling. In the Ten of Pentacles, the woman is in front of her mirror, trying to decide which of her many necklaces, earrings,

The Ten of Pentacles from *The Pagan Tarot*

or other personal ornaments she will wear that day. I could appreciate the humor in an average Witch's predilection toward the acquisition of too much pagan paraphernalia and jewelry as the final pip card in the earth element series.

The back design of this deck is a monochromatic green design of a male and female, both robed initiates, standing together with the four Elementals circling them. This is a one-way design, and would have to be ignored if the reader regularly uses reversals in their readings. Considering the detailed and divergent renderings on the cards, the reader would need to be sufficiently familiar with this deck before using the deck with reversals.

Nevertheless, there is much to recommend this deck to pagan practitioners. It expresses a singular viewpoint of contemporary paganism in Western culture. This deck includes features of modern life like cars, computers, grocery stores, and office settings. It is singular to find a deck that correlates to events of daily life.

A Closer Look At:

Faery Wicca Tarot

Created by Kisma K. Stepanich
Illustrated by Renée Christine Yates

- 83 full-color cards and a 180-page minibook in a slipcase

- Cards are 4¾ x 2¾, with nonreversible backs and illustrated pips

- Vivid images use scenes and characters from Irish mythology to illustrate the journey of the tarot

- Includes four extra "Faery Journey" cards to enhance readings and meditation

- Companion book contains retellings of Irish myth and legend, and several new spreads designed specifically for the *Faery Wicca Tarot*

Three of Domhan

Ainnír of Aer

19- The Sun Child

7- The Chariot

Six of Tine

Ship of Fools Tarot

reviewed by Elizabeth Genco

The *Ship of Fools Tarot* is the last of several decks to spring from the sharp mind and playful spirit of Brian Williams. Artist, art historian, expert on all things Italian and Renaissance, Brian was well known and loved in the tarot community. His extensive knowledge of tarot, especially that of the often-overlooked Renaissance-born decks, was a welcome addition to the plethora of information available on their occult successors. The *Ship of Fools Tarot* was Brian's final project, published shortly after his death in April 2002.

The deck consists of cards based on images from a fifteenth-century German literary text, *Das Narenschiff*, by Sebastian Brant. Though now obscure, *Das Narenschiff* ("Ship Of Fools") was quite popular in its day, translated into several languages and arguably the first international bestseller. The book consisted of lessons against all manners of foolery, admonishing its readers to forsake temptation and instead take Brant's idea of the moral high road. Dramatic parallels to many of tarot's archetypal images are found in *Das Narenschiff*'s woodcut illustrations; as such, the cards of the *Ship of Fools* deck are in most cases lifted directly (redrawn by Williams) from the text or have only minor additions or changes. Those few remaining cards without direct *Das Narenschiff* counterparts have

The Vagabond from the *Ship of Fools Tarot*

0 THE VAGABOND

been carefully composed from the book's sources, often to coincide with traditional *Rider-Waite-Smith* images.

The most striking upshot of the exclusive use of *Das Narenschiff* imagery is that the entire deck is composed of, well, Fools. There's no getting away from the Fool as "Everyman" here; don't be surprised if you find yourself discovering new insights into the model of the tarot as "the Fool's Journey" when using this deck. The influx of Fools infuses the cards with a playful spirit, one that advises us to not take life so seriously all the time. "Those few people who can't appreciate the Fool probably need his influence most," Brian reminds us, a lesson made especially plain by virtue of the deck's inherent irony: that it is a deck of Fools composed entirely of images from a book that vehemently advises us not to be fools. Such a paradox might take some getting used to, but in the end Brian pulls it together brilliantly. I often felt when using this deck that I was the one having the last laugh at some cranky fifteenth-century guy, which, I must admit, is its own kind of big (albeit a bit dorky) fun.

With a few exceptions, the deck ascribes to the familiar *Rider-Waite-Smith* keywords and structure. Given the deck's Renaissance influence, the structural switch of Justice and Strength from the *Rider-Waite-Smith* positioning makes sense. The attempt to allow for wands and swords to correspond to either fire or air (to allow the user to work with whatever they're most comfortable with) doesn't quite come off, however. Brian admits that he's a swords/air wands/fire sort, and these correspondences are evident in the given keywords. I would advise anyone using this deck to just go ahead and use those correspondences.

Most divination meanings provided are traditional, but some are dramatically different (the Eight of Swords as a "directionless journey" or "a mission or crusade," to take one example). For the most part this is all well and good, but for a few of the cards with more moralizing images (such as the Queen of Pentacles), the variations on traditional meanings are odd enough to be distracting. Overall, the book is fairly light on divinatory meaning, which might prove difficult to those who are in the early stages of their tarot practice. On the other hand, fewer and simpler meanings allow for greater intuitive interpretation, which others might find a strength. Nonetheless, a clear attempt to be consistent with the *Rider-Waite-Smith* system was made here, and anyone familiar with that deck should have few problems reading with this one. That the *Das Narenschiff* images are short on some of the tarot's denser occult symbolism adds to the deck's accessibility.

13 DEATH

Death from the *Ship of Fools Tarot*

The deck's artwork consists of line drawings in brown ink on cream-colored stock, straight out of *Das Narenschiff*'s fifteenth-century woodcuts. No additional color is used. I found the color scheme to be a lovely change of pace (and certainly appropriate given the aesthetic of the deck); however, those who draw on color symbolism in readings will find themselves out of luck. Brian stayed vehemently faithful to the woodcuts when redrawing the cards, only changing the artwork to add tarotcentric details (such as extra pip items like wands or pentacles). In many cases (especially throughout the Trumps), he made no changes at all. When composing new images for the (surprisingly) few cards that needed

EIGHT OF SWORDS

The Eight of Swords from the *Ship of Fools Tarot*

them, one can barely tell that they didn't come straight from the source (except, of course, for the fact that most of those images, not coincidentally, look just like their *Rider-Waite-Smith* counterparts). A subtle improvement that Brian doesn't mention but, I imagine, he must have taken into account, is in the faces of the Fools and others in the deck. They're much softer and easier to look at than the *Das Narenschiff* images—something I came to appreciate the more I worked with the cards.

The accompanying book is the one place where the *Ship of Fools Tarot* falls short for me. Those accustomed to Brian's dense, detailed texts may very well be disappointed. Most of his customary art history information is missing. Descriptions of cards are short, both in length and on detail; often they consist of visual comparisons of symbolism on the cards to that on the *Tarot de Marseilles* and the *Rider-Waite-Smith* deck, all of which is easily gleaned from observation (pictures of both are included throughout the book). Details on the reasoning behind the choices of symbols, or information on them, would have made for a much richer text. I often found myself wanting more: more information, more reasoning behind some of the choices made, etc. Overall, the book feels more like a missed opportunity than an addition.

The *Ship of Fools Tarot* is a fun deck and a fitting, upbeat end to a distinguished tarot career cut tragically short. Brian's bright heart and spirit are here—I dare you not to smile when using this deck! These cards remind us that a little Foolishness is indeed a good thing.

The Gilded Tarot

reviewed by Diane Wilkes

A s webmistress for Tarot Passages (www.tarotpassages.com), I see and review many decks. While I try to approach them as an Everyreader, the truth is that few mainstream tarot decks excite me—at least, not in the sense that I'll actually use them more than once or twice. I tend to be drawn to collage decks like *Transformational Tarot* and the *Blue Rose Tarot*, because I find that their often complex and evocative multilayered symbols and artistic metaphors engender deeply nuanced, profound readings.

When I first saw the *Gilded Tarot* online, I mentally dismissed it as an overly stylized reworking of the *Rider-Waite-Smith* (RWS) *Tarot*. A mass-produced deck published by Llewellyn Worldwide, the *Gilded* seemed pretty and accessible, but also vacuous and soulless, much like the nymphet who doesn't know who Aretha Franklin is in Steely Dan's song, "Hey Nineteen."

Despite my initial reservations, the *Gilded Tarot* cards seduced me almost immediately. I admit to being a pushover for cards with black borders and backdrops, but I was also drawn to the colors. They snap, crackle, and pop with the intensity of an entire box of Rice Krispies.

But beauty alone isn't enough to turn my head. What matters most to me is the images' evocativeness quotient, also known as "how the deck reads." And that is the area where the *Gilded* really shines. Every reading I've had with this deck has provided almost glaring illumination, messages with pointed depth and accuracy. What I give up in nuance, I gain in crystal clarity. The *Gilded* even has a sly sense of humor: in one reading, the card representing the individual actually included the person's name. And when I was procrastinating about writing this review, I pulled a card for enlightenment as to why and received the Four of Cups, reversed. Talk about a literal and straightforward message: "Get off your lazy, daydreaming butt and put that mental review on paper!"

Interestingly, deck artist Ciro Marchetti knew almost nothing about tarot prior to being approached by Llewellyn to create a deck, so if you're looking for a deck laden with esoteric symbolism, you've come to the wrong location. However, Marchetti based the *Gilded* on the Golden Dawn–based *Rider-Waite-Smith* deck, which has esoteric symbolism to burn, so there's only one degree of separation. And, of course, if you're familiar with the *RWS*, there is no learning curve involved with the *Gilded Tarot*.

Let's look at the cards themselves, beginning with the Fool, which reflects this deck's strengths and weaknesses in one fell swoop. The image is of a jester balanced precariously on a baton festooned with shiny ribbons, juggling the signs of the zodiac. The background is a dreamy blend of hues, evoking a misty and magical dusk where a large Full Moon's imposing presence acts almost as a central character in the scene.

The Fool from *The Gilded Tarot*

There's a wonderfully active feel to this card; you can practically see the Fool dancing back and forth as he manipulates the astrological glyphs. The weakness? The signs are out of order. Now it could be argued that the signs are jumbled intentionally, evidence of the chaos engendered by this Uranian spirit. And the Empress card's golden glyph of Venus is certainly apropos. But the Gemini-ruled Lovers are swimming in mighty Piscean-like waters and the Wheel's astrological circle is also out of order. The astrological wheel underpinning the Sun card seems particularly gratuitous.

This suggests to me that Marchetti's attempts to integrate astrology into his artwork are more for occult appearance than well-conceived symbolic content.

Ironically, the deck stands alone and best on its own merits, perhaps because it is modeled after a Golden Dawn–styled deck. The *Gilded* is only weakened by the meaningless metaphysical embellishments that Marchetti occasionally tosses into the mix. The artist would have done well to heed Alexander Pope's words: "A little learning is a dang'rous thing; / Drink deep, or taste not the Pierian spring." The High Priestess evinces the greatest strengths of the *Gilded*, precisely because it is quite different from its *RWS* counterpart. A crescent Moon, long associated with this card, illuminates a naked figure that rises from deep and mysterious waters. This vital revisioning of a card that is often quite static focuses our attention on the fluctuations of the Moon in a profound and unique way.

Another unusually vibrant card (and my favorite in the deck) is Marchetti's rendition of Temperance. A woman garbed in filmy orange floats in the ethers, changing water into fire. Judging by the rapturously intent look on her face, she, too, becomes one with the process and the flames. And isn't that what alchemy is all about? Self-transmutation?

The Minor Arcana has some additional strengths (and weaknesses). While the *RWS* Aces each contain a hand reaching from a cloud, indicating a gift from the divine, the *Gilded* Aces move the power into human hands—literally, in case of the Ace of Wands, which makes one think of man "creating" fire.

Each of the Minors is bordered in gold, with a jewel-like oval of color reflecting the Ace of the suit. The colors don't always equate to the cards' traditional assignments. The suit of Cups, normally associated with the color blue, has an orange oval more reflective of Wands, which is assigned ruby red. The emblems for the Wands and Pentacles are a bit strange; the Wands look like expensive brass pens with a half-hoop earring on top and the Pentacles are five-sided gold shields that occasionally make me think of Godiva Chocolate boxes. But the vibrant card backs are more enticing: the

SIX OF SWORDS

The Six of Swords from *The Gilded Tarot*

jewel tones practically wink at you to get your attention.

The iconography is strongly based on the *RWS*. The Three of Wands shows the ever-present man-overseeing-the-horizon-which-includes-ships-at-sail. The Six of Cups depicts two children in an idyllic scene of overwhelming sweetness. Yet there are differences that allow for nuanced interpretations: in the *Gilded* Three of Wands, the boat is a lot closer to shore in this version, indicating that a project might be in an earlier stage than in its *RWS* counter-part, and the children are the same size in the *Gilded* Six of Cups, which suggests a more equal relationship than its *RWS* equivalent.

I particularly like the Six of Swords in this deck: a blue-robed woman guides her vessel over blue waters under a Full Moon, and even the shape of the boat makes me think of Morgaine returning to Avalon. The serenely beautiful woman in the Nine of Pentacles garden could be your all-too-Martha Stewart-like neighbor (if your neighbor dresses like a Renaissance Faire denizen, that is).

The card characters look like actual people because Marchetti uses real-life models. While the *Gilded Tarot* art is computer-generated, the artist draws (or paints) the images using a digital pen and tablet. His software enables him to select the brush sizes, shapes, and colors he wants and the combination of graphic and personal art makes for striking images that breathe. However, this can be unfortunate, as in the case of the Two of Cups, where the two glowing faces resemble members of Abba, a group I prefer moribund.

The companion book, written by Barbara Moore, reminds me of her beginner's tome, *What Tarot Can Do For You*, with its breezy style and modern approach. In *The Gilded Tarot Companion*, she offers exercises to help the novice become comfortable with the cards, as well as short card interpretations and five spreads, from basic three-card layouts to the Celtic Cross.

Visually, the book is a true companion for the *Gilded*, with its consciously artistic style. Selected images from the cards, such as the lion's head from the Strength card and the trumpet from the Judgement card, are scattered throughout the pages, which adds to its trendy, eye-catching look. While I find the book interesting and attractive, it's only 150 pages, including several with blank lines provided for journaling purposes. If Llewellyn had made this set a minikit, it would have been more portable and economical for tarotists on a budget.

When I read professionally, I offer clients a choice of decks. Every time I have made the *Gilded* an option, the querent has chosen it without fail. I have found that men, in particular, are drawn to this deck. Maybe they are suckers for black borders, too? This deck is slick as spit—but I mean that in a good way. Right now it has become a favored tool in my tarot-reader's arsenal, because of its seemingly universal appeal to querents as well as its direct and articulate readings. Will I be as infatuated with it a year from now? It remains to be seen whether its attractions will last the test of time, but at present I am inclined to view the *Gilded Tarot* as a classy number—more like the song "Hey Nineteen" than the empty-headed Lolita the song describes.

Temperance from *The Gilded Tarot*

The World

Spreads

IL MONDO
LE MONDE
XXI
THE WORLD
EL MUNDO
DIE WELT
DE WERELD

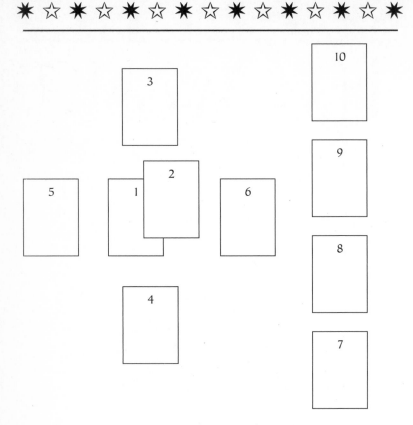

The Celtic Cross Spread

This is one of the most common and useful spreads for divining potential outcomes.

1. The querent
2. Influences on the querent
3. Message from higher self
4. Foundation of the question
5. The near future

6. The far future
7. The querent's fears
8. The querent's environment
9. The querent's hopes
10. The final outcome

✳ ☆ ✳ ☆ ✳ ☆ ✳ ☆ ✳ ☆ ✳ ☆ ✳ ☆ ✳

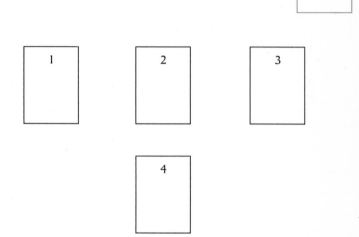

Freeze Frame Spread

The predictive aspect of divination can be overrated. Past and present are eternally fluid and intangible—all we really ever have is the "now." This is a great way to take a snapshot of that now.

      1. Where you are coming from

      2. Where you are now

      3. Where it looks like things are going

      4. Foundation, or source of strength

      5. The next turn of the Wheel (optional)

—by Thalassa

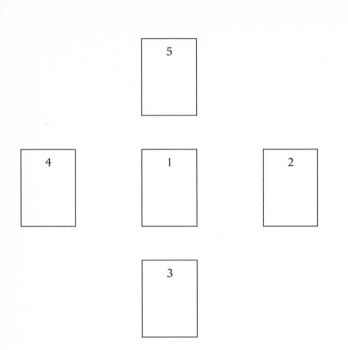

Who Am I? Spread

This is a general spread to help the querent ground and center before a reading begins.

    1. How the querent feels about him- or herself

    2. What lies in the querent's heart

    3. How the querent is affected by others

    4. The querent's biggest fears

    5. Obstacles in the querent's path

—by Bonnie Cehovet

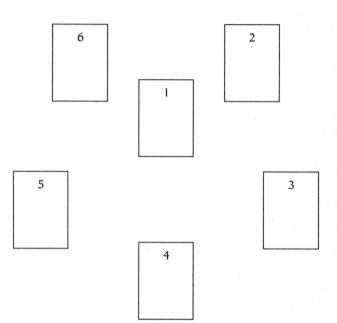

Heart's Desire Spread

1. Your heart's desire (chosen deliberately or at random)
2. What helps you
3. What hinders you
4. What supports you
5. Your next course of action
6. Warnings for your journey

—by Elizabeth Genco

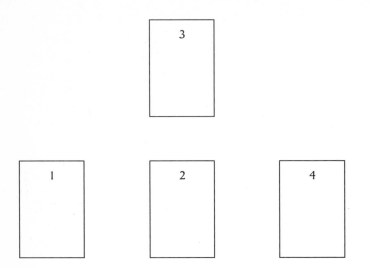

Over the Hurdle Spread

This spread is useful when you need quick insights into how to solve a problem, approach a challenge, or overcome a creative block. Want to supercharge your problem-solving session? After generating one solution, deal new cards into positions 3 and 4 . . . and repeat the process as many times as desired.

1. Your original goal

2. The obstacle you've encountered

3. A strategy for revising your goal or jumping over the obstacle

4. The benefit of taking this new approach

—by Mark McElroy

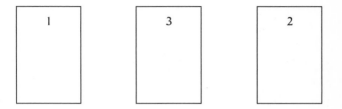

Reality Check Spread

In many situations, we work ourselves into a knot by imagining the worst. At other times, we're unrealistically optimistic. The Reality Check layout addresses such moments, providing best- and worst-case "what ifs," then giving the true nature of the situation. Knowing these three points of view puts the situation into clearer perspective.

> 1. The worst-case scenario (conscious or unconscious) in your mind/imagination about the situation
>
> 2. The best-case scenario (conscious or unconscious) in your mind/imagination about the situation
>
> 3. The reality of the situation itself

—by James Wells

✴ ☆ ✴ ☆ ✴ ☆ ✴ ☆ ✴ ☆ ✴ ☆ ✴ ☆ ✴

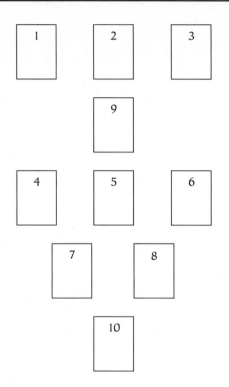

Strength and Love Spread

This spread is appropriate to use when there are critical events or tests in the future of a relationship, or when you need to explore the aspects of a changing relationship. Cards 1 through 8 are dealt normally, while cards 9 and 10 are drawn at random.

1. Visible current situation
2. Querent's current inner self
3. Hidden current situation
4. How the situation will evolve
5. Developing thoughts/emotions

6. Hidden elements
7. Results of efforts
8. Unexpected results
9. Card of Strength
10. Card of Love

—by Elizabeth Hazel

✶ ☆ ✶ ☆ ✶ ☆ ✶ ☆ ✶ ☆ ✶ ☆ ✶ ☆ ✶

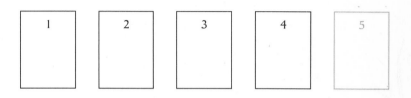

Tarot Toolbox Spread

When I'm finished reading, I like to create what I call a "Tarot Toolbox"—a little packet of information to help the querent remember the reading. It's a great way to answer the question, "Well, what do I *do*?"

1. Air: What you need to do about your mental landscape
2. Water: What you need to deal with emotionally
3. Fire: What you need for focus, drive, and passion
4. Earth: What you need to do in the material world
5. (Optional) The overarching factor, the spiritual aspect

—by Thalassa

Notes

Notes

Notes

Notes

Notes